EQUANIMITY
Conquering Mt. Entrepreneur

The Og Mandino
Leadership Institute

Foreward by "Famous Dave" Anderson
Member: Entrepreneur Hall of Fame

Prologue by Steve Morris
Founder, EXIT Realty

OgPress

Equanimity: Conquering Mt. Entrepreneur
The Og Mandino Leadership Institute

Library of Congress Cataloging-in-Publication Data
Equanimity: Conquering Mt. Entrepreneur / The Og Group, Inc.
Library of Congress Control Number: 2017933254

ISBN 978-1-60645-183-0

Book Cover Design: Christa Reed
www.christareedphotography.com

Book Interior Design: Francine Eden Platt, Eden Graphics, Inc.
www.edengraphics.net

Illustrations: Patrimonio Designs Limited
www.retroclipartz.com

Published by

OgPress

www.ogmandino.com

Author's Second Edition First Printing

PRINTED IN THE UNITED STATES OF AMERICA

DEDICATION

WE HAVE BEEN GIVEN THE FIDUCIARY RESPONSIBILITY of bringing Og Mandino's work into the 21st Century. He set a firm foundation for teaching these principles. It's with great deference and reverence that we continue his legacy. Thank you, Og.

To our 100,000+ courageous clients who have allowed us to step into their world and address the real issues that impact success, happiness, and peace of mind, thank you. You have validated the sheer resilience in the human spirit even when placed under extreme life circumstances. It has been such an honor to serve you.

To our coaches who trusted the process and in turn have become products of the process, we thank you. Each day when the sun goes down, we know the world is a better place because of your dedicated service.

To all who have read early drafts of this book and provided encouragement, thank you.

To our very creative cover designer, Christa Reed, our visionary layout designer, Francine Platt, and our meticulous editor, MarNae Washburn, we give a special thank you.

To our spouses and children who have been so willing to make personal sacrifices so this work would continue to move forward, we express our deepest appreciation.

TABLE OF CONTENTS

Equanimity (ekwə' nɪməti): Peace of Mind

I N 1968, Og Mandino's first book was published. It was entitled, *The Greatest Salesman in the World*. It soon became a bestseller. Over the years, twenty-five million people in twenty-five different languages have purchased this book. It has become one of the best selling self-improvement books of all time.

In the book we find *The Ten Scrolls*. The scrolls came in a single event—an inspired twelve-hour download. Speaking of that experience, Og would later say, "I simply took dictation." We might add—on his trusted IBM Selectric typewriter. Time-tested and battle proven, these principles continue to inspire millions of aspiring leaders.

It would have been about 6:00 a.m. when Og penned Scroll IX: *I will act now*. Pause for a moment and hear the keys of his typewriter as his fingers transcribe the inspired words flowing into this heart, to his mind, to the crisp clean sheet of paper.

My dreams are worthless, my plans are dust, my goals are impossible. All are of no value unless they are followed by action…

…My procrastination which has held me back was born of fear and now I recognize this secret mined from the depths of all courageous hearts. Now I know that to conquer fear I must always act without hesitation and the flutters in my heart will vanish. Now I know that action reduces the lion of terror to an ant of equanimity [peace of mind]. *I will act now…*

…I hunger for success. I thirst for happiness and peace of mind. Lest

I act I will perish in a life of failure, misery, and sleepless nights. I will command, and I will obey mine own command. I will act now.

It is time to turn the lion of terror into an ant of equanimity. It is time to satisfy your hunger and thirst for success, happiness, and peace of mind. *Equanimity—Conquering Mt. Entrepreneur* is YOUR journey. Discover how to create your dreams in tangible reality—profit with a purpose. You are the main character. Be courageous, live the journey. Discover your *Equanimity*.

FOREWORD

"*Famous Dave*" *Anderson is America's Rib King—Founder of Famous Dave's of America, Inc., and Old Southern BBQ Smokehouse. He started his first business in the basement. From those humble beginnings, he created a chain of barbecue restaurants that have been recognized by Nation's Restaurant News, in March 2013, as America's Best Loved BBQ restaurants.*

Dave is the recipient of numerous other awards including Oprah's prestigious Angel Network award and in December 2012, was inducted into the National Entrepreneur's Hall of Fame along with Fred DeLuca, Founder of Subway, Truett Cathy, Founder of Chick-Fil-A, and Sarah Blakely, Founder of Spanx. This highly successful entrepreneur was in the bottom half of his high school class but has earned his Master's Degree from Harvard University without an undergraduate degree and has received an Honorary Doctorate Degree for his life's work.

Dave should have been dead three times, has been bankrupt two times, has gone through treatment and has been sober for 22 years. Through it all, as Zig Ziglar wrote, "Dave turned his backyard grill into a $500 Million Restaurant Empire!" So far as an entrepreneur, Dave has played a critical role in the creation of three publicly traded companies and the creation of over 20,000 new jobs—and he is still creating.

As Dave will share, "My greatest treasure is my wife and sweetheart, Kathy. My greatest accomplishment is our 45 year marriage and beautiful children."

Hi! THIS IS DAVE ANDERSON. I am a serial entrepreneur. Most of my growing up years, I thought I was the dumbest kid in class. I didn't need anyone to tell me because it was painfully obvious. However, all that changed back in 1971, the day I got my hands on a little paperback book entitled, *The Greatest Salesman in The World*, written by my good but late friend, Og Mandino.

I would have been a lost soul, never realizing my dreams if not for Og and his writings. Og awakened my soul to possibilities, supported my recovery and sobriety, and changed the trajectory of my life. I can seriously say, "I don't think I would be successful today if it weren't for the Scrolls, which I continue to repeat over and over to this day. "

In moments of deep discouragement, known by every entrepreneur, I have wanted to give up, but revisiting the Scrolls always lifted my spirits and refueled my courage to persist until I succeeded. This gift is so profound in my life, I have given the book to over 5,000 people, many of whom are high school and college students. I wanted to give them the same gift of inspiration.

I think my life as an entrepreneur is proof-positive that anyone, no matter where they come from or what they've been through, can create success. All you need is a willingness to learn principles, work hard, and live a life obsessively devoted to making others successful—creating happiness. The best thing of all, you don't have to be rich, smart, or have all the answers to start. My own story proves this.

So many people struggle, living paycheck to paycheck, fulfilling someone else's dream. This is unfortunate because almost everyone in their younger years had a dream of starting their own business. Perhaps you started a business—a lemonade stand, mowed the neighbor's lawn, or had a paper route. Unfortunately, the principles of entrepreneurship are taught to children only in a few select private schools. Most never have formal educational opportunities to learn how to start and run a successful business.

I sincerely believe that everyone has within them one idea that could become a game changer, one that could create value for millions and make the world a better place. Others love to serve and share products and services others created, but choose to own the same vision. Bring your unique vision to Mt. Entrepreneur. This book is for you and anyone who is serious about actually creating their dreams.

In today's world of high drama, negativity, and insecurity, it is so difficult to be positive about one's future. Under the pressures of life, too many let worthy dreams fade into escape and avoid fantasy or catastrophe, wrecking any chances for creation. As Entrepreneurs we can't be whimpering sissies or escape artists. We must be dreamers—visionaries—filled with unwavering hope and aspirations—and supported by passion-driven action.

How can you do this? How can you take your vision and create it? Take this journey. Discover how to conquer Mt. Entrepreneur and find equanimity. Discover how to create your dreams and create peace of mind!

As entrepreneurs, we want to know how to become the architects of our own destiny. We want to know how to have an unwavering mindset filled with clarity, hope, and determination. We want to know how to create a vision that ignites passion and drives action. We want to know how to intentionally create our dreams in tangible reality. We want to know how to succeed in today's highly competitive and unforgiving marketplace. You have found it. You are here ready to pull into the parking lot at the base of the mountain. You are ready to get out of the car and climb. You are ready to discover what it takes to summit.

Og's writings helped me understand that *Entrepreneurship* is not a job or a profession—it is a lifestyle, a way of being. The latest book, *Equanimity—Conquering Mt. Entrepreneur*, from The Og Mandino Leadership Institute, assists us all in actually climbing the mountain we call entrepreneurship. Make the first three critical decisions every aspiring entrepreneur wants to make before beginning this journey. Then take the journey. Learn and begin mastering the principles found in three progressively important mile markers. In only a few pages you will find your *Self* at the base of the summit ready and willing to conquer the last great obstacle leading to success. You will leave the journey ready to create your dreams—actually create them.

No matter where you currently are on the journey—new or seasoned—the journey up Mt. Entrepreneur is for you. This is especially true if you are struggling with a painful setback. Entrepreneurs never fail. Failure is simply a new starting point for the next attempt. Arm yourself with these principles and courageously climb. Your time has come!

Entrepreneurship is all about *creation*—creating opportunity and value where none existed before. Entrepreneurs live to create *value* even beyond that which is expected. This separates us from the sea of sameness. Read *Equanimity—Conquering Mt. Entrepreneur* and choose to become one of the rare ones.

Entrepreneurship, big or small, is the backbone of America's Free Enterprise System. I am an Entrepreneur. Most of us are aware of the *schooled* definition for entrepreneurship. Here's a fun one. High earning entrepreneurs are often former C-students who had a hard time coloring within the lines. They are often rule breakers and risk takers—unafraid to take on their own fears and tackle the challenges of the world. They are doggedly determined and driven. Sometimes they are aggressive and sometimes they are more like a volcano—calm on the outside but with a fire burning deep down inside. It's not unusual for entrepreneurs to struggle with addictions—substance abuse, food, or work. It's not unusual for us to have ADHD and struggle with details and structure. Some even have a lot of traffic tickets because they are always in a hurry.

Did you say, "WOW!!! That's me!" Yes, anyone can be an entrepreneur IF they are willing to stretch and grow, crash, and then stand and create again! Become an entrepreneur!"

I am very open that God facilitated the changes in my life. Today I live a life of gratefulness and sobriety. My greatest treasure is my wife and sweetheart, Kathy. My greatest accomplishment is our 45 year marriage and beautiful children.

If you want to start a business or you are already in business but struggling to make sense of today's accelerated and ever-changing marketplace, I urge you to devour *Equanimity—Conquering Mt. Entrepreneur*. It has been crafted in way that *YOU* get to be the main character. This is your journey. Be courageous. Learn how to create your worthy dreams and enjoy the greatest gift of all—equanimity—peace of mind.

— "FAMOUS DAVE" ANDERSON,
JANUARY 2017, HAYWARD, WISCONSIN

PROLOGUE

As Founder and Chairman of EXIT Realty Corp. International, Steve Morris is a true visionary. His years of experience in the Real Estate industry began in the mid 70's. He has been awarded countless designations including Top Sales Manager in North America, and Top Broker/Owner for multiple offices from one of the largest franchise organizations in the industry.

Prior to real estate, Mr. Morris worked on the floor of the Toronto Stock Exchange for several years and was also employed in the cosmetics and insurance industries.

Bringing all that experience to bear at EXIT Realty, Mr. Morris is at the forefront of a new paradigm that has changed the landscape of the real estate industry. His innovation of the EXIT Formula brings added integrity to the real estate business. The Canadian government has recognized his efforts. EXIT Realty Corp. International was also honored by the International Business Awards, a global business awards program honoring great performances in business (also known as the "Stevies"), and earned a Distinguished Honoree medal in the category of "Most Innovative Company of the Year in North America"

Steve Morris travels across North America educating, inspiring, mentoring and leading both EXIT Realty Associates and members of the real estate industry at large and is truly respected for his inspiration and generosity.

IN 2012, I faced the greatest physical challenge of my life. I had already enjoyed a 30-year career in the real estate industry building a successful franchise model and company with hundreds of offices and thousands of agents across the U.S. and Canada and now, I was facing a different kind of challenge.

On vacation in August of that year, my wife Cathy invited me to join her in climbing Gros Piton, the taller of the two majestic mountains located on St. Lucia's southwest coast. Climb a mountain? On vacation? I was turning 66 years old that week. I try to keep myself in good shape (I wasn't blessed by my genetics) but Cathy is a champion who works out daily and is, for all intents and purposes, a mountain goat. I am not. What I am, however, is competitive. No part of me would be able to live with her having climbed the mountain without me so I agreed to accompany her—on my birthday.

When the day came, we made sure we had a seasoned guide who grew up playing on the mountain, the right equipment, and we were mentally prepared (or so I thought) for the climb ahead. Gros Piton is 2,619 feet high, tree covered, volcanic rock and the climb is made at a steep angle. It rained three times that day causing the moss-covered rock to become slippery and treacherous. Every muscle in my body screamed on my way to the top. I know, I counted 18 screams. By the time we summited, I experienced utter physical exhaustion.

We were told there would be places to rest along the way but the third rest stop was the point of no return. It was there we had to make the decision to call it quits and wait for the others in the group to complete the climb or to continue on and not look back. Isn't it the same in business and in life? There comes a time when, in order to reach our goal—in order to conquer Mt. Entrepreneur—we have to let go of all that is familiar and forge ahead fueled by the courage of our convictions.

As we climbed I couldn't see the summit so it seemed like a never-ending journey. I was supremely focused on only the next 20 feet. To take a wrong step could result in a terrible accident. Finally we reached the top only to be told the journey down would be even more difficult.

During the descent I used an entirely different muscle group and about half way down, my feet became numb and I started to doubt my abilities. Doubt triggers fear and I questioned my ability to make it down safely. Doubt can be eliminated with good, positive input and consequently I became immersed in positive self-talk, focusing solely on my next step. I was living only in the present moment. Our guide recognized that I was the weak link in the group and he took special care with me coming down the mountain.

An empathetic mentor is worth his or her weight in gold and mine was with me, literally, every step of the way, telling me where to position my feet, which branch to hold, but as good a mentor as he was, he couldn't make the ascent or descent for me. That was my challenge to tackle, my doubt and fear to overcome.

That day I learned what it meant to draw on every fibre of my being, to go through tremendous pain and self-doubt, to summon endurance where there was none, and climb anyway.

Regardless of how successful one becomes in their career as an entrepreneur there are times when they once again become the student relying on the teaching, training and coaching of others. Realizing this was one of the finest experiences of my life.

Standing at the summit of Gros Piton was not the most valuable experience that day. I suppose I could have hired a helicopter to drop us at the top so we could enjoy the pretty view but then I wouldn't have benefitted from the lessons I learned along the way. I wouldn't have learned what I was capable of doing during the grueling climb. With that discovery came equanimity—a very special kind of peace of mind.

Equanimity—Conquering Mt. Entrepreneur, reminds us that, "The journey tests a person's mettle revealing both the dross and the gold." Enjoy the journey. Have the courage to reveal your gold.

I wish you safe travels.

– Steve Morris, Founder,
EXIT Realty, February 2017, Toronto, Canada

Arriving at the Parking Lot

IN THE EARLY HOURS OF MORNING, we pull our car into the parking lot. We lean forward and look up straining to see the summit of Mt. Entrepreneur. "It looks a bit taller than expected," we nervously muse as our heart pounds, fed by alternating surges of excitement and uncertainty.

We again rehearse the instructions given, "It's simple. All you have to do is read the first section of the book, drive to the parking lot early tomorrow morning, park, and meet us at the trailhead. And, yes, bring the book with you."

We quickly glance over at the book sitting on the passenger seat and then back to the business at hand.

"This place is jammed with cars," we mutter under our breath as we look for an open stall.

Suddenly two people step out right in front of us. We slam on our brakes. "Whoa," we say aloud while shaking our head and smashing the horn on the steering wheel.

Wearing Hawaiian shirts, white linen shorts, and flip flops, and pulling colorful suitcases packed and overflowing, it's clear these two are preoccupied—oblivious—and impervious to the early morning chill. They didn't see our car, so what are the chances they cared to look at the weather report?

"Thunderstorms and freezing temperatures tonight," we mumble.

It's then we have a flash. We see our *Self* on the side of the mountain, sleeping in a tent, weathering the pending storm. This visual sends a little chill down our spine. Still a little unnerved by the Hawaiian Surprise, we continue our search for an illusive parking space.

We see taillights.

"Yes! A parking angel!"

We slow down as the car backs out of the stall and pulls forward. We wave as the car passes, but there's no response from the unshaven, stoic, and ragged looking driver.

We shrug it off and pull into the welcomed empty space. Coming to a stop we put the car in park, shut off the engine, look around to get our bearings, and proudly and audibly proclaim, "Well, I'm finally here!"

Excited to step out and look around, we reach for the door handle and look up just as two people approach the car parked next to us. A man is limping badly and a woman with her arm around his waist is assisting.

Instead of opening our door, we roll down the window and ask, "What happened?"

The question causes the couple to pause. They respond, "Did you just get here?"

"Yes," we answer.

"Then you don't want to know."

We watch as the passenger door is opened and the injured man prepares to sit. We notice a copy of the book resting on the seat. The man picks it up and summarily tosses it in the back seat.

A little puzzled, we glance over at our copy of the book and then at the trailhead. We see people excitedly starting on the path and some departing. Far too many of those leaving look cold and defeated.

We turn back as the car carrying the injured passenger begins to back up. We continue watching until it pulls away.

Increasingly anxious, we take a quick glance at the other cars in the parking lot. It's then that we notice something very odd. One car has roots growing through its tarnished chrome wheels. Another is beat up and covered with dirt as if it had been sitting in a junkyard for decades. Yet another is missing tires and rims and is resting on cinder blocks.

Inside the cars we see people. In one, the driver has his hands glued to the steering wheel and is staring at the mountain. In another, two people are clearly in an argument. Yet another, an extra large pizza is being delivered and money exchanged.

One car in particular catches our attention—two adult occupants in the front seat and two children in the backseat. The car has fogged windows. It is sitting in the parking lot as if frozen in time. Just then, a child closest to us turns, and with a wool mitten, clears a small circle in the glass. We make eye contact, smile, and wave. The child returns the wave while forcing a smile.

Without breaking our gaze, we instinctively reach over to the console, grip our Yeti mug filled with hot chocolate, take a quick sip, and simultaneously give the child one nod of our head. The child acknowledges and turns away.

The bizarre scene is very different than expected and it leaves us with a visceral feeling that *all is not well*.

Sitting alone in our car, which is parked less than a hundred feet from the trailhead, we can feel our enthusiasm, excitement, and confidence begin to wane.

We glance over at the book resting on the passenger seat. The instructions were clear, "Read the entire first section before commencing the journey."

Truth? We haven't even opened the cover. Considering what we have already encountered, we decide it might be wise to at least peruse a few of the pages.

The book is entitled, *Equanimity—Conquering Mt. Entrepreneur.* We can barely pronounce the word "equanimity" without assistance from Google. We pick up the book and with curiosity and a little trepidation open it and begin reading.

— SECTION I —

Welcome to the Parking Lot

O g Mandino writes, *"I am not on this earth by chance. I am here for a purpose and that purpose is to grow into a mountain, not to shrink to a grain of sand. Henceforth will I apply all my efforts to become the highest mountain of all and I will strain my potential until it cries for mercy."*

We see a map with an "X" delineating our location and continue reading.

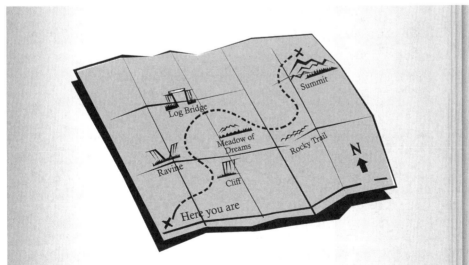

Conquering Mt. Entrepreneur is divided into three sections. In the first, we clearly define what makes an entrepreneur an entrepreneur—why they are different?

In the second section, we address the first three critical decisions every aspiring entrepreneur will want to make before commencing this journey. Our level of commitment regarding these decisions directly impacts the level of our success.

Having made the first three critical decisions, we get out of the warmth and comfort of our car, open the trunk, check supplies, put on our hiking boots, strap on our backpack, and walk over to the trailhead. Be on the lookout for a mentor that can walk by your side.

Og Mandino writes: *"My dreams are worthless, my plans are dust, my goals impossible. All are of no value unless they are followed by action. I will act now!"*

We want to be ready and willing to do whatever the mountain asks of us.

We pause and again look around at all the people sitting in their cars. They appear to be so stuck.

Feeling a sense of urgency, we continue reading...

The third section is dedicated to the three mile markers we discover during our climb. To find them, we place our feet on the path and begin the journey of conquering the mountain. As we approach each mile marker, carefully read and digest the principles and practices provided.

As we climb, we will get ample opportunities to practice these principles. Application will give us new insights and wisdom. As we apply and begin the journey of mastery, the climb becomes steeper but increasingly instinctive and more joyful even during thunderstorms. We also become increasingly aware and prepared to avoid alluring pitfalls that would otherwise sabotage our efforts.

Og writes: *"I will avoid despair but if this disease of the mind should infect me then I will work on in despair. I will toil and I will endure. I will ignore the obstacles at my feet and keep mine eyes on the goals above my head, for I know that where dry desert ends, green grass grows. I will persist until I succeed."*

We can feel a spark of excitement and continue reading.

Having acquired ever-increasing levels of ability to handle ever-increasing levels of difficulty with ever-increasing levels of confidence and ease, we set our sights on the summit. We are starting to use our gifts to ignite passion and drive focus, discipline, effort, and action. We have increased confidence in our ability to climb even the most technical and difficult sections of the path. We have also proven our ability to survive and even thrive in the most challenging of weather conditions. Grateful for the wounds now healed and lessons now learned we are ready to summit.

Og continues, *"Failure no longer will be my payment for struggle. Just as nature made no provision for my body to tolerate pain neither has it made any provision for my life to suffer failure. Failure, like pain, is alien to my life. In the past I accepted it as I accepted pain. Now I reject it and I am prepared for wisdom and principles which will guide me out of the shadows into the sunlight of wealth, position, and happiness far beyond my most extravagant dreams until even the golden apples in the Garden of Hesperides will seem no more than my just reward."*

Faced with a Herculean task similar to the one referenced by Og, and more than aware that Hercules was a mythical character, we nevertheless feel a heightened level of confidence rising up from a place in our being we have rarely dared to visit. This feeling reignites our commitment to press forward.

We turn the page and read about *The Refiner's Fire*.

The Refiner's Fire

The decision to become an entrepreneur is one of the most courageous and rewarding life journeys a person can take. Those who have chosen this way of living confirm—the journey tests a person's mettle, revealing both the dross and the gold. Those who choose this refiner's fire—the rare ones—become the builders of people and the creators of dreams—the true alchemists of our time.

Momentarily looking up and glancing around the parking lot, we raptly whisper, "I want to become one of the *rare* ones."

We continue reading,

Each day thousands of people around the world make the decision to leave the apparent security of a job and a regular paycheck, or the relative comfort of home, and travel to the mountain. Sadly, some never leave their cars. Others get on the trail with backpacks filled and overflowing with unrealistic expectations only to be crushed by a landslide of reality. Others, more determined and driven, hike part time, but for only short distances up the path. They hunger and thirst for a time when they can climb for longer periods of time and to greater heights.

Then there are the full-time hikers, all in, ready and willing to do whatever is required to conquer the mountain and summit.

For a moment we pause to ponder.
Then turn the page and read about *Individual Missions*.

Individual Missions

Individuals come to this mountain for very different reasons—different missions. Some may want to start a practice such as a nurse practitioner, doctor, accountant, or attorney. Others may want to sell real estate, securities, or insurance. Some may want to start a service business or open a retail store. Yet others may want to be coaches or consultants. Many want to build a home-based business. All want a better life.

We pause and ponder our mission—our purpose for coming to the mountain.
More excited than ever about the possibilities, we continue reading,

The financial, educational, and credentialing requirements for each mission vary—some dramatically. Rule of thumb: The lower the barrier to entry—the more important it is for an aspiring entrepreneur to fully understand and consciously make the first three critical decisions.

We quickly flip to pages deeper in the book hoping to discover the three critical decisions but decide to be patient for the time being.
We turn to the next page and read about *The Baseball Bat of Life*. The title of this section catches our attention.

The Baseball Bat of Life

As we all are at times beat up by the baseball bat of life and left wanting life to be easier and a little less stressful, we may be tempted, or sadly, even persuaded to view this journey as an easy path to a winning lottery ticket—a less stressful life with lots of time and financial freedom.

We may be tempted to use our entrepreneurial gift of visualization to engage our mind and vivid imagination in fantasy, all in an effort to escape and avoid our current reality. Early in the morning and late at night, and, all too often, during the productive hours in the day we may play out in our mind vivid scenarios about a peaceful, easier, and less stressful life *after* we summit the peak.

To support these mental movies, we may dutifully make elaborate dream boards and compose long-winded superfluous affirmations believing these words will facilitate magical manifestation.

We call this alluring yet hollow and vapid process the Millionaire Magic Doctrine of Manifestation. This doctrine focuses on having, getting, receiving, and arriving, not on the real journey, which focuses on stretching and growing—becoming and creating. At the core of this doctrine is a belief that if we visualize with enough intention, our dreams will be magically manifest without needing to do the work of climbing Mt. Entrepreneur.

Sadly, those who succumb to this doctrine end up disillusioned and even angry. They want linear time to speed up and everyone to show up at that speed. They demand the universe somehow magically manifest their dreams. After all, they asked and visualized with real intense intention. Sadly and far too often, this was the instruction. Left sitting in their car in the parking lot, circumstances unchanged, fantasy not manifested, they pound on the steering wheel in frustration.

Faced with the inevitability of "needing" to get out of their car and climb the mountain—do the work of creation in order to realize their dreams—they find the very thought boring, mundane, repetitive, burdensome, and hard, requiring motivation that is not present and effort that is unsustainable.

In time, they begin to beat themselves up, **"I can almost touch it. I can almost taste it. Why can't I have it? What is wrong with me?"** and even, **"Does God not love me?"** In the end they are left devastated.

When the avalanche of debt crashes down, they leave the parking lot broke, broken, and angry singing *The Hype and Hopeum Blues*. It is as if their dreams have been cut out of their hearts with a dull knife. This outcome is both tragic and unnecessary.

We again glance at the people stuck in their cars and notice those who are in fact pounding on their steering wheels, obviously shouting, but clearly unheard by man or the universe.

We introspectively realize, "Sometimes I want life to be easier and less stressful." With a subtle gulp we ask, "Do I ever engage in escape and avoid fantasy?"

Willing to explore but uncertain of the answer, we turn the page to *The Power of Visualization* and continue reading.

The Power of Visualization

Entrepreneurs do not want to escape and avoid, they want to engage in life, embrace obstacles, connect and serve others, create value, and contribute to the world. They want to leave a footprint on this path.

Instead of spending valuable and productive time playing escape and avoid mental movies in their minds about what it will be like *after* they summit, entrepreneurs use their gift of visualization to get a clear vision of where they want to be—the summit—and the steps required to reach it successfully.

The reason? Visualization manifests inspired ideas, intuitive impressions, and creative solutions that ignite passion. Passion is the gift they are given to sustain the work of creation—climbing—stretching and growing—becoming and creating. Passion-driven, entrepreneurs climb without counting the cost or tracking the time.

Interestingly, an entrepreneur most likely has a dream board tucked away in their backpack, but instead of it being a fantasy facilitator, it is utilized as a clear target. It stands as a constant reminder of where they are headed and why they are willing to pay the price to take the next step and create the next millimeter.

They also have affirmations, but instead of being banal platitudes focused on wishing, wanting, receiving, or getting, they are focused on being, becoming, taking action, and creating.

Let us emphasize, entrepreneurs first focus their gift of visualization on the summit. Armed with a clear vision of where they are headed and driven by passion they commence the journey. As they climb, they continue to use their gift of visualization to get additional inspired ideas, intuitive impressions, and creative solutions to tackle the daily *tests of courage* and the *challenges to their commitment*. They view each step as a *creation completed* and the foundation for the next step. As a result, they stay on the path and stay focused on climbing.

Bottom line: Visualization is a tool by which entrepreneurs manifest vision and gain clarity, which in turn ignites passion. It is not used to facilitate fantasy.

Entrepreneurs know that visualization does not manifest tangible reality, action does. When used constructively, visualization ignites passion, which drives and supports action.

The natural outcome of creation is joy in the journey and equanimity—peace of mind. Entrepreneurs do not frantically chase money because they know it runs. They instead focus on service and creating value. When they do, money flows.

We reach for a pen and write in the margin, *Stay focused on my vision and the next step on the path. Stop chasing money.*

We continue reading.

Entrepreneurs cannot distinguish the difference between creation and relaxation—hiking and sightseeing—because they are always on the path that leads to success even when relaxing and in every other part of life. The process of creating—the journey—lights up their soul.

What a stark contrast between those sitting in their cars in the parking lot, pounding on their steering wheels out of frustration, wanting their dreams to be magically manifest versus the passion-driven entrepreneur who intentionally climbs to the summit one step at a time—vision and passion-driven—growing and stretching and becoming all they were meant to become. Which one do we want to be—the one sitting in the car trying to cash in on a fantasy lottery ticket or the inspired, passion-driven, equanimity filled climber?

We spontaneously respond, "The inspired climber!" We are excited to begin this journey—even a little antsy.

We turn the page to *Ultimate Freedom* and continue.

Ultimate Freedom

Entrepreneurs think outside the box. At the core, they resist structure that doesn't make sense. They want freedom to create!

"Amen," we shout aloud. "Yes!"

They have also learned, and often the hard way, that structure does not have to be viewed as confining and restrictive. When it supports the creation of our dreams it becomes instead a beautiful invitation to freedom—ultimate freedom.

Conversely they understand, the freedom to resist, resent, and rebel is not freedom at all. It is instead a cleverly disguised trap that robs us of ultimate freedom.

This section causes some reflection and we ponder, "I've been resisting and resenting structure and rebelling against rules for a lifetime. I've never viewed structure as an invitation to freedom — ultimate freedom. Hmmm…"

Entrepreneurs find hierarchal environments and controlling relationships restrictive and suffocating—impediments to their potential and roadblocks to the creation of their dreams. Therefore when selecting mentors, they value competency and contribution versus a person's rank, title, or credentials.

"Absolutely," we say aloud.

Entrepreneurs are constantly thinking about new and better ways to do everything—a creative gift. However, they often get attached to their ideas, need to be right, and when they do, run the risk of crushing people along their path. If we gathered together all our companions, families, and close friends and asked them the following question what might the answer be? Do I ever have strong opinions about the way things need to be done?

After a brief pause and truthful review, we respond, "Of course. Rhetorical."

With a slight chuckle we turn the page and begin reading, *My True Self*.

My True Self

Entrepreneurs burn through fear and self-doubt like it is fuel for the soul. Instead of choosing to be swamped by life and burdened by procrastination, they embrace challenges along the path and see each as an opportunity to become stronger and more capable so they can climb higher.

Og writes: *"Only action determines my value in the market place and to multiply my value I will multiply my actions. I will walk where the failure fears to walk. I will work when the failure seeks rest. I will talk when the failure remains silent. I will call on ten who can buy my goods while the failure makes grand plans to call on one. I will say it is done before the failure says it is too late. I will act now."*

We again turn and glance at the trailhead and then up at the peak. The early morning sun is glistening off the ragged rocky peak.

The excitement we initially felt when considering whether or not to come to the mountain is returning, but it's already different— somehow deeper.

"If that's what this journey is all about, I'm all in," we whisper with determination.

We continue reading,

When asked to address and serve their very best clients and customers, entrepreneurs show up on their very best behavior. They understand this is their true, genuine, and authentic *Self*. They are not faking it. They are instead being aware of the needs of others and consciously shutting off any noise—unhealthy habits of thinking—that would otherwise detract or distract.

They understand that because of unhealthy habits of thinking, it may be difficult to sustain this heightened level of awareness when faced with difficult challenges and during moments of stress and fatigue. They want to be conscious and aware more often and for longer periods of time.

They understand that the common desire to *let our hair down* simply means we no longer want to fight our unhealthy habits of thinking and therefore are surrendering our free will to them.

Entrepreneurs want to bring the best version of their *Self* to each and every moment, and most importantly, home to those they love the most.

"Never thought about it that way," we consider as we bring an index finger to our lower lip. "I always thought that was faking it."

Still thoughtful, we turn to *Pivotal Moments of Improvement* and continue reading.

Pivotal Moments of Improvement

Entrepreneurs are like sponges—they read from the best books to expand horizons, think without limitations, and courageously act without hesitation. Not knowing what to do next—what step to take—is simply an invitation to figure it out.

Entrepreneurs understand that self-improvement has more to do with the application of knowledge than the accumulation of knowledge. When they read books, engage in coaching, attend trainings, webinars, and seminars they understand it is for the purpose of preparing for private pivotal moments along the path in which they consciously choose to maximize natural strengths and change unhealthy habits of thinking.

They know self-improvement occurs in these pivotal moments—while in action—while climbing to the summit—and based on conscious decisions, shaped by wisdom gleaned, but made while in the middle of these moments.

Entrepreneurs understand that the brain has neuroplasticity—it is malleable. Each time they choose to replace an unhealthy thought with a healthy one, they begin to create and then strengthen a new neuropathway—a new habit of thinking.

For an entrepreneur, self-improvement is not about being wrapped in a warm and fuzzy blanket or having their mind coddled with vapid, banal, or intellectual aphorisms. It is not about circumstance or manipulation. It is a very real experience of raising consciousness, and then in pivotal moments along the path, choosing to replace old unhealthy habits with new and healthier habits.

James Allen writes (*As a Man Thinketh*): *"Let a man radically alter his thoughts and he will be astonished at the rapid transformation it will affect in the material conditions of his life."*

Nodding in agreement we conclude, "Change my thoughts and this is what will change my circumstances. I like that."

We turn the page and read about *Dark Nights.*

Dark Nights

Lastly, entrepreneurs know dark nights—moments of doubt, confusion, fear, inadequacy, and near total exhaustion. In these moments, they are uncertain if they have the strength to take another step, slay another dragon, or overcome another setback or disappointment. Somehow and from a place deep in their souls—a place every successful entrepreneur knows intimately—they find a modicum of hope, an inspired idea, a little reminder of where they are headed and why their dream is so important. With this comes a purging of their doubt and a reigniting of their passion.

These are the defining moments of every successful entrepreneur. Each will tell us, "The remarkable decisions made while in these caverns of catharsis refined my vision, reignited my passion, and elevated the trajectory of my success."

"Amen to that!"
We conclude this section by reading, *The Rare Ones*.

The Rare Ones

These are a few of the reasons why an entrepreneur can awaken each day unemployed ready to take on any challenge or fear—the house they live in, the car they drive, the clothes they wear, the food they eat, and the opportunities available are all dependent on a clear vision, deliberate daily actions, and the results intentionally created…and they are always seeking to improve this sequence by jettisoning unhealthy habits that impede creation.

In short, entrepreneurs have a clear vision of where they are going, work passion-driven, live in the now, slay dragons, encounter obstacles, make mistakes, reevaluate, learn from their experiences, make adjustments, and intentionally create—take the next step—and then do it all over again.

When they summit this peak of success, they are prepared and ready to assist others in their climb. They can't help it. For them, the freedom to create is like breathing air and the joy in the journey as valuable as the outcome. They would never trade this for the apparent security of a predictable paycheck.

Are you ready to start your journey?

"Ready? Yes!" we exclaim.

What seems to *just happen* for this rare segment of the population starts with three critical decisions. These decisions are foundational. **When absent, a person may step out of the car and get on the path dragging a suitcase packed and overflowing with unrealistic expectations only to be hit by the landslide of reality in the first half mile.**

We quickly glance up to see if Mr. and Mrs. Hawaiian shirts have started up the path. They are nowhere in sight. The very thought of what they will shortly face causes us to grimace.

When this happens, some realize they are better suited for the structure and predictable compensation model of traditional employment and return to the workplace. They often become more dedicated and effective entrepreneurial employees—creative, self-directed, and totally accountable. If their current culture is unsupportive, they often seek employment elsewhere.

Others are simply shocked by the raw reality. They exit the path and willingly leave behind their dreams of a better life. They need less pressure and less stress. They willingly settle for mediocrity.

Others never leave their car in the parking lot or quickly return after only a short jaunt. They end up hanging out in the parking lot a bit too long pretending to be entrepreneurs, carelessly borrowing and spending money they can never pay back. Burdened by unhealthy expectations they invest in one expensive program after another in search of a magic pill—a way to magically manifest their dream of summiting without climbing.

We again glance around the parking lot at all the people still sitting in their cars. We are beginning to understand. "Very sad," we gently whisper.

Entrepreneurs—the rare ones—discover real joy comes from learning and patiently applying the laws that govern the creation of any worthy dream—and in taking the steps along the path. They begin climbing the best they can with the strength they have. In doing so, they discover new reservoirs of strength—natural gifts they did not know they had—and acquire new abilities learned along the path. In addition, people are put on their path who can serve them and whom they can serve. New vistas—new opportunities—open to their eyes. They experience equanimity.

They soon discover that when preparation—maximizing current strengths and acquiring new ability—meets opportunity, miracles unfold—not magic—miracles.

To this end, we encourage all who want to hike this path to make the first three critical decisions, commit to mastery, and then walk over to the trailhead and begin the journey. Whether choosing to be an entrepreneur full-time or part-time, when engaged, we want the freedom to create—ultimate freedom—and with a willingness to pay whatever price is required to secure it. In time, Mt. Entrepreneur is summited and while on the journey our dreams are intentionally created.

This book is an invitation to become one of the rare ones—a true entrepreneur. The journey begins by making the first three critical decisions.

"What are the three critical decisions?" we impatiently ask.

We quickly turn the page to the second section of the book. We are finally there—*The First Three Critical Decisions.* Excited, we continue reading.

The First Three Critical Decisions

O g Mandino writes, *"I ask not for gold or garments or even opportunities equal to my ability; instead, guide me so that I may acquire ability equal to my opportunities."*

As entrepreneurs we will want to make three critical decisions before commencing the journey up Mt. Entrepreneur. These decisions can be applied to the creation of anything—a great relationship, a successful business, personal health and well being, and more.

While reading consider the following question:

Have we ever made a total commitment to something or someone? This would be a commitment without excuses. One free from trap doors, safety nets, and escape routes—a *burn the ships*, no turning back kind of commitment in which the only option was to press forward and create success.

As we read and face each of the three critical decisions consider the following:

In the past, how often have we wanted life to be easier and less stressful and fallen victim to fantasy?

In the past, how willing have we been to settle for the freedom to resist, resent, and rebel against structure—even the structure that creates the success we desire?

How badly do we want ultimate freedom?

Lastly, in what ways would our life be more successful, joyful, meaningful, and fulfilled if we viewed commitment as an invitation to freedom, embraced it, and did whatever was required to keep it?

Feeling a little hungry we pause for a brief moment to reflect on these questions. We reach into the glove box and retrieve an energy bar, tear open the wrapper, take a healthy bite, and while chewing, again glance around at the people still sitting frozen-like in their cars.

We reflect on the frustrations experienced when we want life to be easier and less stressful and it keeps showing up differently. We reflect on the difference between ultimate freedom and the freedom to resist, resent, and rebel and how this has shown up in our life. It's not really funny, but our past behavior causes us to smile and cathartically chuckle a little.

We reflect, "Am I ready to acquire new abilities?"

Question left unanswered for now, we turn the page, settle in, and begin reading *The First Critical Decision*.

The First Critical Decision

Should we ever become unhappy or overwhelmed in our current career path or job and begin the search for something better and more fulfilling, we may look out the window of Corporate America or through the windshield of our car and spot a successful entrepreneur. On what might we focus?

We might want to believe that entrepreneurs have a lot of time and financial freedom because they are out and about apparently *playing* in the middle of the workday—and desire this freedom. We might notice their enthusiasm for life, a warm smile, and bright countenance—and hunger for this level of success, happiness, and peace of mind. We might focus on the material trappings and toys—and dream about having these possessions. On what else might we focus when enticed by the idea of becoming an entrepreneur? After all, entrepreneurs seem to have the very things we secretly admire and desire."

We quickly glance up at the cars in the parking lot.
Returning to the book,

> Because of fatigue, disillusionment, and even boredom we
> may at first be tempted to over-focus on these perceived out-
> ward benefits. Should we, it may be difficult to see and thus
> understand what truly drives the entrepreneur and fully appreci-
> ate the price they are willing to pay to focus this *driver* on the cre-
> ation of their dreams. Furthermore, we may not have taken into
> consideration this *driver* when exploring our own secret desires
> and real intentions for wanting to become an entrepreneur.

We take another bite of our energy bar and continue reading.

> This underlying *driver* is the most important piece of the puz-
> zle and the one most often missed when weighing the options
> and considering the possibilities. Yet when we do understand
> and appreciate this essential piece—this *driver*—we may dis-
> cover that it is even more exciting than any desire for an easier,
> less stressful life—and when awakened, more fulfilling.

Curious, the thought causes us to shift our body position a little.
We continue reading,

> A true entrepreneurial soul hungers for the freedom to cre-
> ate. They want their lives and their ideas to matter and want
> the freedom to act on these ideas without needing approval or
> permission. They want to invest their time creating these ideas
> in tangible reality.

Introverted or extraverted, entrepreneurs create connection and trusted relationships. They are good listeners and seek to create value in the lives of others.

Entrepreneurs are creative and self-directed. They want to, get to, and choose to do the next right thing for the right reason.

Their independent natures, disruptive ideas, and dogged determination are not always compatible or even welcomed in heirarchical business environments or controlling relationships.

In short, the driver is a burning desire to create while being totally responsible for their actions and fully accountable for the outcome—no trap doors, safety nets, or escape routes.

Og Mandino writes, *Within me burns a flame which has been passed from generations uncounted and its heat is a constant irritation to my spirit to become better than I am, and I will. I will fan this flame of dissatisfaction and proclaim my uniqueness to the world.*

Og continues, *Today I will surpass every action which I performed yesterday. I will climb today's mountain to the utmost of my ability yet tomorrow I will climb higher than today, and the next will be higher than tomorrow. To surpass the deeds of others is unimportant; to surpass my own deeds is all.*

Our mission in this moment is to assist all who are considering the challenge of summiting Mt. Entrepreneur to awaken this *driver*—this flame. We believe it is fundamental and foundational. We also believe it is inherent in those desiring to take this worthy journey, although often masked by the *wet blankets* of fear, self-doubt, shame, and blame—the natural consequences of secretly wanting an easier, less stressful life, and engaging in escape and avoid fantasy.

Can we feel this flame—this irritation down deep in our gut—this insatiable appetite to be more and create more—this desire to live fully, serve completely, make a difference, and leave a footprint on this planet?

We take another quick sip of hot chocolate while pondering the question.

Is this *driver* alive and well and roaring in our soul or has it been nearly suffocated by fear and doubt or a desire for ease and less stress? Is it nearly extinguished by the energy required to play life half-speed—one foot on the brake, one on the gas?

Do we have any fear about what might be required? Have we been avoiding this moment wanting a little break from the rigors of life? Based on past experience, are we concerned about losing our *Self* in the process? Are we feeling a little anxious, unworthy, or incapable? Have we been so beat down by life that we want to be magically transported to the summit? AND at the same time has there been a knowingness that this flame is calling to us wanting release? Can we hear its call? Are we ready to fan the flames of dissatisfaction?

How many programs have we purchased or workshops attended? How many books have we read? How many coaches have we engaged while searching for another and less stressful or less scary way to the summit? What has been the result thus far from our efforts to avoid this moment of decision?

Did we ever in our wildest dreams or fantasies imagine that it was in the embracing of this driver—this flame—we

could finally find our *Self* on the path that leads to success, happiness, and peace of mind—not ease—but peace?

Are we ready to let go of the need for ease, rip off the wet blankets of fear and doubt, stoke the embers, breathe in life, and reignite the flame? Are we ready to take the actions and embrace the structure needed to summit Mt. Entrepreneur?

"Yes," we shout aloud, quickly looking around to see if anyone heard our outburst.

We live in a world that seeks an *Easy Button*. At one time or another, most people have wanted one. It even makes for great humor in TV commercials. However, and as we all know, we don't live in commercials. Interestingly, we already own the most valuable easy button. It is very different than the one the world might try to sell us, but nonetheless we have all flirted with it on special occasions.

Og Mandino writes, *"My procrastination, which has held me back, was born of fear and now I recognize this secret mined from the depths of all courageous hearts. Now I know that to conquer fear I must always act without hesitation and the flutters in my heart will vanish. Now I know that action reduces the lion of terror to an ant of equanimity* (peace of mind). *I will act now!"*

What happens every time we procrastinate and then finally shut off the noise in our head and jump in and tackle a task? What do we normally say to our *Self*? Go ahead. Say it out loud.

"That wasn't so hard? Why did I wait so long?" we instinctively whisper.

Every time we do this what shows up? Every time we shut off the noise in our head and jump in, our flame—this *driver*—our true Self—free of fear, self-doubt, shame, and blame shows up! It is so magnificent even we are surprised! "*Wow*, that wasn't so hard. *Wow*, why did I wait so long?"

How long have we been playing this game with our *Self* and our flame—avoid, avoid, avoid, delay, delay, delay, jump in—SURPRISE! Avoid, avoid, avoid, delay, delay, delay, jump in—SURPRISE!?

"All my life," we admittedly murmur.

Is it time to stop being surprised? Is it time to push *this* easy button? Is it time to rip off the wet blankets and add fuel to the flame—to jump in once and for all—all in—and be totally committed?

It is time! It is time to be real and create great relationships; it is time to be genuine and awaken our natural genius and bring it fully to the service of others; it is time to be authentic—our true self—instead of playing small and going half speed; it is time to embrace our flame, our intrinsic driver.

If we are truly ready to reignite our flame and awaken our natural genius, if we truly want the freedom to create—ultimate freedom—let's start by making the first critical decision: *I choose to become the Boss.*

Wanting to become an entrepreneur does not free us from having a boss. It demands that we instead become the boss.

"Become the boss? What does that mean?" we ponder.

> The decision to become the boss is the defining pivotal moment that separates fantasizers who want their dreams to be magically manifested from entrepreneurs who are hungry to create their dreams in tangible reality.
>
> When we choose to become the boss we are saying, this is my life and I am responsible for what I do with it. In the past, I resisted, resented, and even rebelled against the very structure that supports success. *Today, I begin a new life.* Today I choose differently. I choose to embrace and fan my flame. I welcome mentors and the wisdom they share, but I do not need any other human being to wake me up in the morning, push me, prod me, or prop me up. I choose to be *Self*-directed—doing the next right thing for the right reason because I want to, get to, and choose to. I choose to become the boss.

We again glance over at the trailhead and then lean forward and look up in an attempt to see the summit. The morning sun is rising over the horizon and peeking through the clouds. Its rays are reflecting off the summit and illuminating the cars in the parking lot.

We glance over at the car with the two children. Even through the fogged glass, the desperation is palpable. We can feel a desire welling up inside to share what we are learning and feeling.

With some desperation, we whisper, "They need this book."

We turn the page and continue reading,

> In one of the darkest hours of his life, Dave Blanchard, CEO of *The Og Mandino Leadership Institute*, remembers shouting aloud, "*I long to cry to the God of my youth, but the God of my*

youth will not hear my cry. I must change my God or change my cry." Buried with a million dollars in debt, exhausted by the rigors of life and in pain, he recalls, "*I just wanted to be rescued."* When it did not come, he simply got angry—and real.

All who share his belief that there is a higher power—Dave calls God—have at one time or another prayed as he prayed for days on end, "*What should I do? What should I do? What should I do?"* Dave shares, "*The answer was much different than expected and a little hard to hear at the time. God simply whispered, 'Do something.'"*

There is no power for good in the universe that will rescue us and rob us of the opportunity to stretch and grow and become. If that has been our cry, it is our cry that needs changing.

When writing our first book, *Today I Begin a New Life— Intentional Creation*, there was one specific morning that is remembered well. As was the norm for the four years invested, it was 4am.

The previous morning the chapters entitled, *Fantasy—the deadly seed,* and, *Catastrophe—the deadly weed,* were completed. Stepping back, the pressing question was this, "*What are we really trying to say?"* That was followed by, "*What's the bottom line, the common denominator? Both the true entrepreneur and the fantasizer share the same powerful gift—the gift of visualization. Why do they use it so differently?"*

The evidence was overwhelming, the answer clear. **For the entrepreneurial mind, the gift of visualization is delicately and precariously balanced on a fulcrum called secret desires and real intentions. Our gift tips one way or the** other—creation or fantasy—depending on the desires and intentions with which we visualize.

If our *secret desires and real intentions* focus on having a life that is easier and less stressful, including the desire to be rescued, our gift tips toward destructive uses such as fantasy and catastrophe (obsessive worrying). As a result, we get trapped in a deadly and debilitating cycle.

While in fantasy, we spend private time and productive hours playing out vivid scenarios about life *after* our dreams are magically manifest—after we have been rescued. We experience euphoria driven by the hormone norepinephrine. We create a new mental construct or new reality in our mind. This creates an expectation—etymologically *a concrete condition for happiness*. In short, an expectation is a non-negotiable mental monolith—something so real to the mind the body will go to war to protect it.

When life shows up differently, and it always does, our sympathetic nervous system releases the stress hormone cortisol, which is designed to heal wounds and speed up metabolism. It is as if an enemy that wants to destroy our new reality is attacking us. We feel anxious at a cellular level.

It gets worse. Our amygdala, our flight or fight center, sends out an army of fear dendrites. Their mission is to conserve the energy needed to flee or fight by shutting down energy rich parts of our brain starting with our prefrontal cortex. This drastically impacts our higher levels of consciousness—empathy, common sense, and practical judgment. We experience a mental brownout and are rendered emotionally paralyzed.

In the end, our fantasy does not magically manifest. Our expectations—our concrete conditions for happiness—are left unmet. We are *left* disillusioned and frustrated with tangible reality—our life. It is in dark moments like these that we cata-strophize—play out worse case scenarios that drive us deeper and deeper into the dungeon of despair and discouragement. Eventually we turn inward looking for blame and engage in *Self*-deprecating dialogue—*Self*-loathing. As shared earlier, it may sound like this, "*I can almost touch it; I can almost taste it; Why can't I have it? What is wrong with me?*" And even, "*Does God not love me?*"

The well-worn solution for this addictive-cycle-gone-bad is to self-medicate by reengaging in fantasy and creating a new release of the euphoric drug norepinephrine. Should we reen-gage, the cycle begins all over again.

This cycle sucks the oxygen out of our flame and when faced with the work of creation, which no one gets to skip, we find it boring, mundane, repetitive, burdensome, and hard. This cycle frequently leads to *burn out*.

Sadly, many who have a desire to become an entrepre-neur secretly desire an easier and less stressful path. It is simply too dangerous should we come to the mountain seek-ing this kind of ease.

"No one has ever explained it like this before. This is crazy," we ponder while considering if and when we have ever experienced similar physiological consequences from fantasy and catastrophe. We conclude we have and it *has* dampened our flame.

On the other hand, if our *secret desires and real intentions* are focused on stretching and growing and creating, our gift of visu-alization tips toward constructive uses. We spend time mentally rehearsing future events wanting clarity and seeking guidance. We explore possibilities without making tangible commitments and, thus, minimize mistakes. We seek inspiration regarding people we can serve based on our unique life experiences, take action, and create deep connections. We problem solve, plan, and set goals, and make commitments that give meaning, purpose, and direction to our daily actions.

As a result, we are rewarded with the manifestation of inspired ideas, intuitive impressions, and creative solutions that literally light up parts of our brain—parts that are normally dormant in humans. This ignites our passion—fans our flame—and we do the work of creation passion-driven.

The next question asked the morning after the chapters on fantasy and catastrophe were completed flowed naturally, *What principles support a secret desire and real intention to stretch and grow and create?* Again the evidence was overwhelming.

There were five. Now, it is time to provide more detail for the hungry entrepreneurial mind.

Believing we have one of these busy minds, we begin reading about the first principle, *Engage.*

Engage

Entrepreneurs choose to live. They want to take the clay they have been given and create the most they can with it. They want more—more of their clay, not someone else's. They want to become the best possible version of themselves. In doing so, they find purpose and joy in the journey of life and in the process of creating a brighter future. Their reward is equanimity.

Og loved metaphors. In one of his most famous, which is found in *The Greatest Salesman in the World, Scroll VIII: I will multiply my value a hundred fold*, Og compared us to a grain of wheat. He suggests we have one of three futures. One, we can be put in a sack, dumped in a stall, and fed to the swine—waste our life. Two, we can be ground into flour, made into bread, broken open, and devoured by the will of others—let others determine our future. Third, we can be planted in the darkness of the soil in order to ripen—to stretch and grow and become all we were meant to be.

Og Mandino writes, "*Now, like the wheat grain, which will sprout and blossom only if it is nurtured with rain and sun and warm winds, I too must nurture my body and mind to fulfill my dreams. But to grow to full stature the wheat must wait on the whims of nature. I need not wait for I have the power to choose my own destiny.*"

Og continues, "*The height of my goals will not hold me in awe though I may stumble often before they are reached. If I stumble I will rise and my falls will not concern me for all men must stumble often to reach the hearth. Only a worm is free from the worry of stumbling. I am not a worm. I am not an onion plant. I am not a sheep. I am a man. Let others build a cave with their clay. I will build a castle with mine. Today I will multiply my value a hundredfold.*"

Let's choose to become the boss and master the principle of engaging in life. Let's choose our clay—no matter how challenging it may be at the present moment—and create the most we can with *it*. There is no power for good in the universe that will give us more of something we do not want. What is the promise should we choose to maximize our clay? When we do, we are given more clay.

We want more clay. We continue by reading the second principle, *Embrace Challenges.*

Embrace Challenges

Instead of resisting or resenting what happens, entrepreneurs see obstacles as opportunities to grow. After all, these obstacles are part of life and can't be avoided so why not embrace them, learn from them, push through them, and move forward.

Og writes, "*I have been given eyes to see and a mind to think and now I know a great secret of life for I perceive, at last, that all my problems, discouragements, and heartaches are, in truth, great opportunities in disguise. I will no longer be fooled by the garments they wear for mine eyes are open. I will look beyond the cloth and I will not be deceived.*"

Entrepreneurs embrace learning, even from obstacles, and apply what they learn. They want to stretch and grow—even when it is unpleasant or uncomfortable.

Entrepreneurs seek to acquire ever-increasing levels of ability to handle ever-increasing levels of responsibility with ever-increasing levels of ease. This is the ease they seek—the ability to create more because they have greater capacity.

Let's choose to become the boss and master the principle of embracing obstacles. Let's always be learning, applying, improving, and performing at the highest levels possible. Growth creates equanimity.

"I can do that," we confidently say aloud as we continue by reading the third principle, *Connect and Serve.*

Connect and Serve

Entrepreneurs are great listeners. They listen to understand versus respond. They know the greatest gift they can give another person is leaving that person feeling understood. This is in contrast to a previous belief that their gift was wisdom and advice.

They find joy in listening, asking empathetic questions, establishing trust, taking down walls of resistance, and creating connection. They understand the greatest secret of success in all ventures is agape love—a heightened level of awareness regarding the needs of others.

Entrepreneurs do not drag around past failures and hurts because it would drain the energy out of everyone around them including themselves. They instead use these experiences as rich empathetic reference points to better understand what others are going through. They hear things few others hear. They see things few others see. They courageously ask questions others might not think to ask. They view painful experiences as their greatest asset.

Og writes: "*I will greet this day with love in my heart. And how will I do this? Henceforth will I look on all things with love and I will be born again. I will love the sun for it warms my bones; yet I will love the rain for it cleanses my spirit. I will love the light for it shows me the way; yet I will love the darkness for it shows me the stars. I will welcome happiness for it enlarges my heart; yet I will endure sadness for it opens my soul. I will acknowledge rewards for they are my due; yet I will welcome obstacles for they are my challenge."*

When we own our life experiences and use them to connect with and serve others, there is finally purpose in our suffering, joy in our journey, and much needed healing in our souls— peace of mind. Let's choose to become the boss and master the principle of connection. Let's become whole and complete so we are more available to serve others. Connection followed by service is a primary source of equanimity for an entrepreneur.

"Hmmm. Sounds right," we whisper as we begin reading the fourth principle, *Create Value*.

Create Value

Entrepreneurs create value everywhere they go and with everyone they meet. They leave everyone happier and every-thing better. As they seek to add value, value is added to them.

Og writes, *"This day I will make the best day of my life. This day I will drink every minute to its full. I will savor its taste and give thanks. I will maketh every hour count and each minute I will trade only for something of value. I will labor harder than ever before and push my muscles until they cry for relief, and then I will continue. I will make more calls than ever before. I will sell more goods than ever before. I will earn more gold than ever before. Each minute of today will be more fruitful than hours of yesterday.*

My last must be my best. I will live this day as if it is my last."

Og continues, *"I will avoid with fury the killers of time. Procrastination I will destroy with action; doubt I will bury under faith; fear I will dismember with confidence. Where there are idle mouths I will listen not; where there are idle hands I will linger not; where there are idle bodies I will visit not. Henceforth I know that to court idleness is to steal food, clothing, and warmth from those I love. I am not a thief. I am a man of love and today is my last chance to prove my love and my greatness. I will live this day as if it is my last."*

Let's choose to become the boss and master the principle of creating value. Let's use every minute wisely creating value and when we are tired, create a nap. Creating value (and taking needed naps) is a great source of equanimity.

"I like naps!" we respond as we continue with the fifth and final principle, *Contribute.*

Contribute

Entrepreneurs want their lives to matter. They gladly give a generous portion of their time and resources to the less fortunate or to other worthy causes. They do so without strings attached yet know it always comes back ten-fold. They want to leave a footprint on this planet. They want to leave it better than they found it.

Og writes, *"Henceforth, I will remember the lesson of the firefly who gives off its light only when it is on the wing, only when it is in action. I will become a firefly and even in the day my glow will be seen in spite of the sun. Let others be as butterflies who preen their wings yet depend on the charity of a flower for life. I will be as the firefly and my light will brighten the world. I will act now."*

Let's choose to become the boss and master the principle of contribution. Let's be generous whether we have much or little. If we do not give now, we will never have enough to give. Discover the equanimity that comes when we contribute.

"Having little—been my excuse for years. Time to let that one go."

As we master each of these five principles our *secret desires and real intentions* will be in alignment with creation. We will receive inspired ideas, intuitive impressions, and a solution that will ignite passion—our flame—and this will drive our actions. We will stretch and grow and create.

Lastly, as we act on these manifestations and spend more time in the Now being our real, genuine, and authentic *Self*, our *Self*-esteem will begin to heal. We become increasingly whole and complete and feel more comfortable in our own skin, and more available to serve.

Clearly, our *secret desires and real intentions* determine how we use our gift of visualization. This directly impacts our ability to make the decision to become the boss AND directly impacts our peace of mind—the equanimity we experience.

Let's choose to become the boss. Let's choose to have *secret desires and real intentions* that support creation. Let's choose to use our gift of visualization constructively to get inspired ideas that ignite passion and drive action.

Choosing to become an entrepreneur is serious business. The journey of *becoming* one is a life choice—a way of living and being. The good news is, no one starts out perfect—just perfectly convicted to *become* an entrepreneur. Start by choosing to become the boss.

Are you ready to go even deeper?

"Yes, bring it on," we whisper with a new found determination as we turn the page to the chapter entitled, *The Second Critical Decision.* We dive in.

The Second Critical Decision

In Corporate America employers hire employees. These individuals are normally hired based on five basic benchmarks: education, skills, experience, drive, and cultural compatibility. In addition to interviews and reference checks, employers often use assessments to determine the suitability of a prospective employee.

A company has a task that needs to be completed, and if and when hired, an employee is expected to complete the assigned tasks in a timely manner and within prescribed quality requirements. If a mistake is made in the hiring process it can be very costly often resulting in a need for additional training or even termination. If the latter, the process begins all over again.

The employer/employee contract is straightforward. The employer gives directions and the employee takes direction. The employer manages the productivity of the employee and the quality of the work product and the employee is accountable for performance and results. The employer is the boss.

Entrepreneurs also hire employees. As the boss, they start by assessing, interviewing, and hiring their single most important employee. This employee impacts for good or for ill every facet of their life—their emotional state, the decisions they make, the actions they take, and ultimately the results they create.

For the entrepreneur, the decision to hire this employee cannot be deferred or ignored. We will want to make this choice before commencing our journey. Success, happiness, and peace of mind hang in the balance. As the boss, it is time to make the second and perhaps the most important of the three critical decisions: *I choose to hire my Self.*

"Interesting," we consider and then continue reading.

Borrowing from our second book, *The Observer's Chair—The Miracle of Healing Self-Esteem,* we read, *As humans we have been given a unique gift, the ability to step back and become aware of our unhealthy habits of thinking—we can become the Observer of our thoughts. This process is called metacognition. Unlike any other living creature on this planet, we can reflect on our own thinking and choose to change the way we think. We can live above and beyond these damaging habits. We can choose to sit in the Observer's Chair.*

"What's this got to do with hiring my *Self?*" we ask aloud. Turning the page we continue.

Have a seat in the Observer's Chair. Firmly grip the armrests and hold them tightly. When we choose to sit here in this chair, we are full participants in life. We are whole and complete, confident, valiant, peaceful, deliberate, and unconditional with our Self. Reflecting on the needs of others we are empathetic, respectful, accepting, tolerant, candid, and compassionate.

This is the place where we receive inspired ideas, impressions, and solutions to challenges—whispers and visions of possibility that ignite our passion and drive our focus, discipline, effort, and action. It is here that we act on our own moral authority doing the next right thing for the right reason because we want to, get to, and choose to. It is here that we find joy in the journey.

It is here we experience success, happiness, and peace of mind. Yes, it is here we learn, apply, and master the principles, practices, and processes that define the Observer—the one who consciously chooses to be an intentional creator [be the boss].

This is a very good place. We know this chair. It feels like home because when we choose to sit here, we are embracing our gifts and proactively choosing our destiny. After all, we are the Observer.

As you sit in the Observer's Chair, notice the other chair over there, the chair of our unhealthy habits of thinking. When we choose to move over and sit in that chair our unhealthy habits of thinking question our worth and worthiness, doubt our ability, and challenge our beliefs and values.

This is where unrealistic expectations are created that foster fear and frustration. This is operation central, the home base of judgment and intolerance, despair and discouragement, over-whelm, and confusion. This is where we feel intimidated, exhausted, impatient, and disorganized. This is where our unhealthy habits of thinking resist, resent, and even rebel against discipline and structure, goodness and light. Sitting in that chair over there, overwhelmed by the incessant noise, we cannot receive inspired ideas or intuitive impressions—hear divine whispers or see visions of possibility.

In that chair over there, our efforts are sabotaged and we are stripped of our freedom and robbed of our hopes and dreams. This is a very dark place. Sadly, we also know that chair all too well.

When we move from the Observer's Chair—our chair—to the chair that belongs to our unhealthy habits of thinking, we surrender our free will—our right to make good choices and wise decisions. We also give up our voice. Yes, we turn our life and voice over to these habits. They are in charge—they run our life—they speak for us.

When we make the choice to sit in that chair over there, we do some crazy things and these deeds truly do threaten to imprison our future. Relationships suffer, productivity is impeded, confusion, and even anger abound—joy is at best elusive.

The operative question at any given moment in the day must always be, "In which chair am I choosing to sit? Am 'I' in this chair—my chair—or have 'I' surrendered my free will and moved over to that chair over there—the chair of my unhealthy habits of thinking?"

"I like sitting in the Observer's Chair," we conclude. "Much more comfortable."

In 1968, Og Mandino's first book was published. It was entitled, *The Greatest Salesman in the World*. In the years since, over twenty-five million people have read the book in twenty-five different languages. The book contains the Ten Scrolls—ten time-tested principles of success.

In one of our favorites, *Scroll IX: I will act now*, Og writes, "*I hunger for success. I thirst for happiness and peace of mind. Lest I act, I will perish in a life of failure, misery and sleepless nights.*"

He then punctuates this burning desire with the following emphatic statement, "*I will command and I will obey my own command. I will act now!*"

This statement addresses one of the most significant principles of success in modern literature—metacognition—the ability to step back and observe our own thoughts. For 1968, Og's statement was revelatory.

"*I will command,*" references me as the boss—my real, genuine, and authentic *Self*, sitting in the Observer's Chair.

"*I will obey my own command,*" references when "I" have wandered over to and am sitting in that chair over there—controlled by "my" unhealthy habits of thinking. When "I" do so, "I" surrender my free will to them. I give them my voice and they speak for me.

Og's admonition translated to common vernacular: "*Hey! Get the heck out of that chair over there and get back in the Observer's Chair. When you're over there, you surrender your free will to those unhealthy habits. You say and do things that are out of character. That's not the real you. "I" am the real you! Rip off the duct tape, shed the chains that bind, I want my voice back. Get back over here in the Observer's Chair.*"

Thus, "I" will command and "I" will listen to my real voice—my true self—and obey my own command and get back in the Observer's Chair. If "I" don't, "I" will perish in a life of failure, misery, and sleepless nights.

"I finally get it!" we exclaim. "When I'm sitting in that chair over there, I'm surrendering my free will. I'm letting my unhealthy habits of thinking speak for me. 'I' will command and 'I' will both hear and obey my command. This is so empowering."

In the past, we may have been unaware that there were two chairs let alone which chair we were choosing to sit in. This is why as an entrepreneur, we first make the conscious decision to become the boss—to sit in the Observer's Chair—and second, to hire my *Self*—become aware when "I" wander over to that chair over there and am controlled by my unhealthy habits of thinking.

The decision to become an entrepreneur, starting with the decision to become the boss, raises the bar of conscious awareness regarding these habits. The journey will fillet us wide open and expose every concern, fear, and personal doubt—our unhealthy habits of thinking. Sometimes it will feel as if they are screaming!

This is good news. Unhealthy habits of thinking have been sabotaging our efforts for years. Before we commenced this journey we may have avoided the discovery or may not have had a strong enough impetuous to become aware. The journey provides this opportunity. It rips off the cover of unconsciousness and lets us finally see. At first, we may not always like what we see.

Please note: Awareness does not create healthy or unhealthy habits of thinking, it simply reveals these habits. Awareness allows us to know where to focus our time, energy, and resources to maximize strengths and make any needed changes. Awareness assists us in focusing our efforts on creating our dreams not on avoiding barriers.

"Do I really want to know?" we ask with some apprehension. We take a deep breath and continue by reading *Unique Thought Processes—Awareness and Management*.

Unique Thought Processes—Awareness and Management

Entrepreneurial souls have very unique habits of thinking. Interestingly, seven of these healthy habits are shared in common 85% to 97% of the time. Four of these habits support high levels of empathy, intuition, common sense, and practical judgment. Three habits support creativity, problem solving, and visualization. These seven unique habits represent what we call *Entrepreneurial Gifting*. All seven have unhealthy and dangerous shadow sides when left unmanaged by the unaware.

The first four habits, when managed properly, support deep connection with others and passion-driven action. Unmanaged, they can talk us out of our own intuition and when faced with difficult tasks they can encourage us to procrastinate.

What kinds of things can impact our management of these first four habits? Here are a few:

- Unmet expectations that rob us of joy
- Practical concerns about our lack of education, credentials, and life or work experience
- Personal concerns about our health, current levels of debt or lack of cash flow, and time availability
- Social concerns—fears about talking to and connecting with people
- Relationship concerns—emotionally or physically abusive companions or deeply challenged children
- Intimate concerns about our worth and worthiness, ability, beliefs, character, and contribution.

The last three habits, which support creativity, problem solving, and visualization are extremely powerful and potentially dangerous if left unmanaged.

As entrepreneurs, we want to be free. We resist structure. We think outside the box unfettered by structure that doesn't make sense. We effortlessly think in search of the best and most effective creative solutions. We manifest inspired ideas, intuitive impressions, and creative solutions that ignite passion.

However, left unmanaged these habits surrender to that chair over there. Instead of resisting structure that doesn't make sense, they want us to resist, resent, and rebel against anything that seems controlling, restrictive, difficult, or hard—including both the people who attempt to impose the structure and our true *Self*.

Unmanaged, these powerful thoughts obsessively churn. We can get attached to ideas, need to be right, and when we do, crush the self-esteem of others.

Unmanaged, we engage in escape and avoid fantasy and

create unrealistic expectations that when unmet foster frustration and drive catastrophizing and ultimately *Self*-loathing.

When we leave the Observer's Chair, sit in that chair over there and surrender our free will, we leave these three habits unmanaged. Left to their own devices, these habits will burn down our own house.

"Ouch! I do that," we admit and then continue reading.

Og writes, "*In truth, the only difference between those who have failed and those who have succeeded lies in the difference of their habits. Good habits are the key to all success. Bad habits are the unlocked door to failure…. I have surrendered my free will to the years of accumulated habits and the past deeds of my life have already marked out a path which threatens to imprison my future.*"

As the boss, let's step back for a moment and examine how we have been using our entrepreneurial gifting:

Do we act on our intuition as if it is an urgent assignment? Have we ever left the Observer's Chair and walked over to that other chair over there and surrendered our free will and allowed our unmanaged habits to talk us out of our own intuition?

"Yes and Yes."

Do we immediately and without delay take on difficult tasks and unleash our natural genius? Have we ever procrastinated and when faced with an immoveable deadline jumped in only to discover it wasn't so hard?

"Yes and yes, again."

Do we embrace structure that leads to ultimate freedom? Have we ever resisted, resented, and/or rebelled against structure that would have served us?

"Sometimes, sadly, and yes, to the rebel part."

Do we look for the good in other people's ideas and create consensus and cooperation? Have we ever needed to be right and potentially crushed the esteem of someone we love?

"Hard to say, but I think I might be a crusher," we admit.

Do we use our gift of visualization to get inspired ideas, intuitive impressions, and creative solutions that ignite our passion and drive our actions? Have we ever engaged in escape and avoid fantasy wanting life to be easier and less stressful?

"Didn't know that was harmful until I read this book," we say attempting to defend past behavior.

Lastly, have we ever left these powerful habits unmanaged—exposed their shadow sides—and are now feeling imprisoned by them due to debt, doubt, and disappointment?

"Cutting a little too deep," we wincingly exclaim.

Which voice is screaming the loudest in our mind? Which voice is the dominant voice? How often are we sitting in the Observer's Chair and how often are we sitting in that chair over there having surrendered our free will?

"Uncle!!" we shout aloud then take a sip from our mug.

It's time. Say it aloud, "I" choose to be the boss and "I" choose to hire my Self. When "I" surrender to my unhealthy habits of thinking, "I" will command and "I" will obey my command and get back over into the Observer's Chair.

We repeat aloud the challenge word-for-word and then continue reading.

When we make the choice to hire my *Self*, we are choosing to become aware of our entrepreneurial gifting. This is the first step in managing and maximizing habits of thinking unique to an entrepreneur.

It's important enough to restate: the vast majority of those attracted to entrepreneurial endeavors have natural entrepreneurial gifting. However, far too many are still sitting in that chair over there burdened by the shadow sides of their gifting.

Let us assist you in becoming more aware regarding which habits of thinking need a little more management.

Somewhat relieved, at least for the moment, we turn the page and read *The Premise*.

The Premise

When Bette Mandino, Og's widow, asked us to take the fiduciary responsibility for bringing Og's work into the 21ˢᵗ Century, we focused first on measurement. For over four decades Og had provided the principles needed to maximize healthy habits and replace unhealthy habits. His work had been time-tested and was battle worthy.

The only question remaining was this: could we find a way to *measure* a person's habits of thinking, the very habits Og had been encouraging us to improve? If this were possible, we could then apply principles, practices, and processes with laser accuracy to maximize impact and speed up the self-improvement process. This would allow our clients to invest their time, energy, and resources more effectively and efficiently to maximize results.

We started with the following premise: Our habits of thinking impact every facet of our lives. These habits either sabotage or support our efforts. Therefore, our habits are foundational to the creation of any worthy dream. We wanted to assist our clients in better managing or replacing unhealthy habits so they could get into the Observer's Chair sooner and stay there longer.

We did not want to focus our time or have our clients invest time trying to manage personalities. We wanted to assist people in becoming the very best version of themselves so they could more effectively and efficiently create their dreams in tangible reality.

"Makes sense," we consider.

Continuing,

This approach required a willingness on the part of a participant to go into a place we seldom allow another human being, let alone go ourselves. It required a willingness to engage in deep introspective and potentially sobering discoveries—to become aware. It required a willingness to be focused, disciplined, and do the work of creating real and lasting change.

Og Mandino was committed to real and lasting change. We had a fiduciary responsibility to stay true to this commitment even if it wasn't the easiest thing to do.

We believed those who would choose to engage could unlock the door to success, happiness, and peace of mind. The big question was, would people choose to commit? This question was particularly poignant when considering our previous discussion around the natural proclivity to resist, resent, and rebel. We had faith those who really wanted to create their dreams—those who wanted ultimate freedom—would engage.

We continue by reading, *Measuring Our Habits of Thinking*.

Measuring Our Habits of Thinking

We found the answer to measuring our habits of thinking in the formal and deductive science of Axiological Mathematics. Instead of using inductive science in an effort to induce a diagnosis—provide a label—identify a personality trait—we chose to use deductive science. This allows us to dive below the surface of personality and measure the very habits of thinking that drive human behavior—the source—the fountain from which we drink in success or failure—our habits of thinking.

Axiological Mathematics, which incorporates Cantor's Transfinite Calculus, provided us with a hierarchy of mathematical value, a baseline from which we could compare and measure how a person values—how they think.

No person or group of persons, no organization political or religious—bottom line—no ideology or theology determined the hierarchy of mathematical value. It was totally objective. It is mathematics. Therefore, there is no moral dilemma around the word, valuing.

Using this math, we could identify with laser accuracy where a person's habits of thinking were in alignment with the mathematical hierarchy, and should they deviate, specifically where and by how much. This allowed us to identify natural strengths, assess deviations, and the level of the risk in these deviations.

Armed with this valuable information, we could apply with confidence the principles, practices, and processes needed to maximize and manage strengths and create any needed shifts.

For the past eighteen years we have focused our energy on fine-tuning this powerful mathematical Assessment tool. We have invested thousands of hours and hundreds of thousands of dollars perfecting the experience of *taking the Assessment*, defining and refining the interpretive data, and the overall presentation of this information.

Our goal was to make this complex mathematical science easier to understand even though humans are quite complex—to the tune of 6.4 quadrillion variables. We also wanted to make the experience valuable, meaningful, and actionable for our clients.

Are people willing to become aware, manage, change, and

improve? For the entrepreneur, the decision to hire my *Self* is critical to success.

When we make the decision to become an entrepreneur our habits of thinking come along for the ride even if we are unaware. When we choose to become the boss and choose to hire my *Self*, we are perfectly positioned and properly motivated to hear, become aware, and do something about it. The creation of our dreams is at stake.

It hasn't always been popular or easy to stick to our commitment of creating real and lasting change but the journey has been worth the outcome.

Although no two people think the same—thus no two assessments are exactly alike—the sheer amount of raw data collected from over 100,000 participants has provided unexpected insights into the mind of entrepreneurial souls.

It has assisted us in identifying thoughts and thinking patterns that if not addressed properly could create serious challenges for anyone who wants to climb this mountain and become an entrepreneur.

It has assisted us in giving guidance to companies regarding messaging that could otherwise trigger unhealthy habits of thinking such as fantasy in large segments of their entrepreneurial population.

It has assisted our clients in using their gift of visualization constructively to manifest inspired ideas, intuitive impressions, and creative solutions that ignite passion while avoiding fantasy and catastrophe.

It has assisted our clients in letting go of the need to be right and in having genuine, authentic, and comfortable conversations that create connection.

The list goes on. The data collected has been priceless.

The Assessment allows us to measure and identify a person's habits of thinking—strengths and challenges—with laser accuracy. It clearly shows our clients where to focus time, energy, and financial resources to maximize their Habit Score. No more guessing. No more generalizations. No more warm and fuzzy blankets, just a clear path with targeted objectives and time-tested results—self-improvement at the fastest pace humanly possible—and with the highest Habit Score.

It's time. Take the FREE Habit Finder Assessment and get your current Habit Score. Let's identify which habits of thinking are supporting your journey and which might be attempting to sabotage your efforts. As the boss, let's conduct a thorough interview with the first and most important hire—my *Self*.

Go to www.HabitFinder.com/book and using the code provided in this book, take the Assessment today for FREE.

"We will later," we say aloud and continue reading.

Recently we were at a client's sales convention. A couple of weeks prior to the event we delivered a presentation via Zoom to hundreds of members from their sales team. They were located all over the country. The topic was *Hire My Self*. Many in attendance at the convention were present on that video call.

At the convention, one of these individuals pulled us aside and asked if we could talk for a few moments. He shared, "I took the Assessment as suggested. After reviewing my results I discovered that I wouldn't hire my Self." This gentleman was a little emotional as he shared.

We said, "Tell us more about that." He did. When he finished we asked for permission to share. We shared, "Now you know which habits have been in the way and holding you back from creating your dreams. Now you can do something about it. This is an exciting moment for you—one of the greatest gifts you can give yourself—awareness of your habits of thinking. Be courageous."

Please take note: Awareness does not create healthy or unhealthy habits of thinking, it simply reveals these habits. Awareness allows us to know where to focus our time, energy, and resources to maximize strengths and make any needed changes.

Entrepreneurs do not want a warm and fuzzy blanket. Engaging in an activity today that feels good is great, but in the long term their singular focus is creating their dreams in tangible reality. They want ultimate freedom. Because of this focus, they are willing to pay whatever price is needed today to ultimately create their dreams in tangible reality even if at first it is a little uncomfortable or even daunting.

Entrepreneurs know that if they want their circumstances to change, they will want to become increasingly aware of and make changes in their internal dialogue—their habits of thinking. They want to have peace of mind even in the midst of a firestorm. If we want life to be better we first choose to become the boss and then choose to hire my Self.

Go to www.HabitFinder.com/book and using the code provided in the book, take the Assessment today and get your current Habit Score. It's FREE. After taking the assessment and getting your results, click on the link provided and schedule a

FREE twenty-minute consultation with one or our certified Og Mandino Coaches.

Take fifteen minutes and complete the Assessment. The mentors on this journey up Mt. Entrepreneur will want to see your results so they can provide appropriate guidance.

"Okay, okay I'll do, it" we respond, anxious to get on with the journey. We pick up our mobile device and log onto www.HabitFinder.com/book, and when instructed enter the code provided. We follow the instructions and complete the *Assessment.*

Surprisingly, it only takes a few minutes and we have immediate access to our results, including our Habit Score.

Our first thought as we review the results is, "How do they get so much information from such a simple process?" Our second thought is, "They nailed me."

"This is getting interesting," we conclude as we again open the book and turn to the page entitled, *The Third Critical Decision.*

The Third Critical Decision

We have made the commitment to become the boss. We have chosen to be self-directed, totally accountable for our actions and responsible for the outcome. We are ready to do the next right thing for the right reasons because we want to, get to, and choose to.

Feeling a little tired, we close the book while marking the page with our right index finger. We stretch, yawn, and glance to our right at the cars in the parking lot. Most of the people are still sitting frozen-like. We glance at our watch. It's already 9 am.

We glance over at the trailhead. We see a young lady being greeted with hugs from several people. They appear to be asking her a question. We lean forward as if to listen. She opens the flap on her backpack and pulls out a book and shows them. They all smile with approval and welcome her on the path. We look down at our copy of the book. Our heart is pounding with exciting to commence the journey and our feet are twitching with impatience.

We hear a sudden loud noise and turn to our left. "What?" A tow truck is hooked up to the bumper of a car, little children still sitting in the backseat. The cigar chewing, greasy-handed operator pushes a lever and the front end of the car rises. The father is standing and begging for mercy. The small child in the back seat again clears the fogged glass and frantically waves.

We quickly roll down our window and shout at the operator, "There are children in that car!" "Look buddy, I work for the bank. Ain't my problem," he shouts in return.

With the flick of his finger, the tow truck driver discards his cigar at the feet of the father, climbs in the tow truck, puts it in gear, and begins to drive away. The father runs to catch up. We quickly open our car door, still holding the book in our right hand.

Leaping to our feet, we shout aloud, "Wait! Wait a minute!" The truck temporarily stops for the father to climb in the passenger seat. The driver pulls away while giving us an obscene gesture with his left hand.

"What a jerk! Unbelievable!"

The truck, car in tow, leaves the parking lot, turns left, and disappears in the distance. From this vantage point we look around at the other cars. It is clear that no one else noticed this brutal repossession.

In frustration, we pound on the top of our car and climb back in our car while muttering, "Come on! This is nuts."

We pause for a moment and take a sip of hot chocolate in an attempt to calm our irritation.

"One more decision remaining and I can finally start climbing!" we exclaim still trying to be calm.

We glance to our left where the car with the small child was once parked. Feeling sad for the child, we turn and continue reading,

> We made the decision to hire my *Self* and with it the commitment to take the Habit Finder *Assessment*. We now know which habits are supporting our efforts and which habits are attempting to sabotage our dreams.

We glance over at our cell phone. For a brief moment we smile as we reflect on the discoveries. Truth is, some of the strengths are a surprise. The challenges? Well, we have been spending way too much time in that other chair so no surprises there—other than we now have clarity regarding specific unhealthy habits of thinking that have been sabotaging our life.

We continue reading,

> We have one last critical decision to make and we are ready to commence our journey. Unlike the first two critical decisions, it's in the climbing that we do the work to support this commitment. It's time to make the decision: *I choose to improve my Self.*
>
> What is the objective... the end game for self-improvement? What are we attempting to accomplish? Yes, we want to bring our habits of thinking into alignment with the principles that govern creation—engage, embrace, connect and serve, create value, and contribute. Yes, we want to manage our entrepreneurial gifting, but it goes much deeper.
>
> Robert S. Hartman, Ph.D., of the famed Hartman Institute

and creator of the Hartman Value Profile, which we use to collect the data for the Habit Finder Assessment, said it best. He writes, "*The Objective is to BE real, genuine, and authentic without the need to impress, pretend, feel shame, or fear.*"

He went on to say, "*This is the most difficult task in our mortal existence and the highest level of maturity.*"

Real is at the root of the word relationship. When we are real we are totally available to connect with and serve others and do so free from self-deprecating and self-centric dialogue. Og tells us that until we master this art we are "*no more than a peddler in the marketplace.*"

Genuine has at its root the word genus or genius. When we are genuine, we bring all of our natural gifts and talents—our natural genius—to the service of others. Should we fail to do this, we rob the world and our *Self* of these gifts.

To be authentic means to be your true *Self*. When we are authentic, we are self-directed, acting on our own moral authority doing the next right thing for the right reason because we want to, get to, and choose to.

Imagine reaching this level of maturity—fully available to serve others, willing to bring our gifts and talents to this service, and choosing to be self-directed. Add to this the absence of a need to impress others so we can feel better about our *Self*—we already feel confident. Add an absence of the need to pretend in an effort to overcompensate for feeling less than—we already feel valuable. Add the absence of the need to cover our gifts with shame, that wet blanket which attempts to extinguish our flame. Instead of dragging around our mistakes we have chosen to learn from them and use them to serve others.

Lastly, add the absence of F.E.A.R.—False Evidence Appearing Real—created by the release of molecules in the body when we obsessively worry. Instead we are courageous and intentional.

This is the endgame of the process called self-improvement. Simply stated, we radically alter our thoughts so we can BE real, genuine, and authentic—being whole and complete, comfortable in our own skin, fully available to serve others, and experiencing a life filled with success, happiness, and peace of mind—equanimity. Should we engage in this level of self-improvement, what is the likelihood we will actively and intentionally identify and create worthy dreams in tangible reality and then create dreams beyond those dreams?"

"Real, Genuine and Authentic," we say aloud as we write these words in the margin.

What is holding us back from this realization? It is quite simple, our unhealthy habits of thinking or when we leave our entrepreneurial gifting unmanaged. This is the reason why we first focus on identifying which habits are supporting or sabotaging this effort, second, focus on managing and maximizing strengths, and third, focus on making any needed shifts.

There are no shortcuts, no lottery tickets for improvement. Books, coaching, webinars, seminars, conventions are not self-improvement, only preparation for the private pivotal moments when we choose to change—when we choose to improve.

We do the changing in these moments—no one can do this for us. This would rob us of the greatest principle in the universe, agency—the right to choose. We can prepare for these moments by intentionally raising our awareness, but the actual decision to change is solely ours.

We may want the world around us to change, but as entrepreneurs we now know if we want our circumstances to change, we start by changing our *Self*, starting with our internal dialogue—our unhealthy habits of thinking or shadow sides of our entrepreneurial gifts.

Attempting to improve our circumstances without making the third critical decision is like trying to climb Mt. Entrepreneur wearing a backpack filled with rocks—some small, some big, all heavy. However, as we consciously choose to change our habits—remove these rocks and discard them—our load becomes lighter, our energy and capacity increases, our ability to see opportunity heightens, and that which was once hard is now much easier and more joyful to perform.

Og writes, *"…and soon these actions and reactions will become easy to perform, for any act with practice becomes easy. Thus a new and good habit is born, for when an act becomes easy through constant repetition it becomes a pleasure to perform and if it is a pleasure to perform it is man's nature to perform it often… Today I begin a new life."*

For some, self-improvement requires a fundamental shift in thinking and a fundamental shift in focus—fantasy to creation, changing circumstances to changing *Self*. The good news is, we can begin the journey up Mt. Entrepreneur while at the same time engaging in self-improvement. In fact the process for creating change becomes even more relevant as we do so.

Some may discover they are addicted to the powerful euphoric drug norepinephrine, which is released when we use our gift of visualization to fantasize. In time, this form of artificial joy can be supplanted by real joy that comes from receiving an inspired idea, acting on it, and creating something of value in tangible reality—something we would not have created if we had stayed in fantasy.

Repeated, this process increases our belief and trust in the principles that govern creation and our willingness to adhere to these principles. In time, we find a new depth in our self-worth, richer connections with others, and a greater sense of meaning and purpose. As a result we are more likely to stay in creation and realize ever greater and more consistent moments of joy— more equanimity.

In explaining these moments, Og writes, "*I will begin to awake, each morning, with a vitality I have never known before. My vigor will increase, my enthusiasm will rise, my desire to meet the world will overcome every fear I once knew at sunrise, and I will be happier than I ever believed it possible to be in this world of strife and sorrow.*"

Enthusiasm is a very powerful word. It references the awakening of our natural entrepreneurial gifting. As our gifts are awakened, we are happier even when standing in the middle of a firestorm. We have equanimity—peace of mind.

Og's words cause us to stop and ponder nearly aloud, "I want to experience equanimity at this level. In the past I've focused on changing my circumstances believing this would bring peace of mind. Nothing ever changed. This is a huge shift in thinking and being."

Slowly at first and then more confidently we speak aloud the words, "I will command and I will obey my own command! I will command…!"

After pausing for a moment to reflect and for our heart rate to regulate, we turn to the page entitled, *Fragile New Habits*, and continue reading.

Fragile New Habits

The world may still experience strife and sorrow, but we are choosing to show up differently—whole and complete—with new and healthier habits. Once a new habit of thinking is created we will want to reinforce it with constant and repeated use until it becomes stronger and stronger. New habits of thinking are fragile. All we need do to break one is drop it.

As we create new habits, we become more and more like our true and authentic *Self*—our most aware *Self*—the observer sitting in the Observer's Chair. Again, we'll want to get here sooner and stay here longer.

The most pressing questions at this point in our journey are these. Do our current habits of thinking encourage and support us in doing the work of creation? Will these habits support us in creating genuine and authentic connections with others? Will they give us a clear vision of possibilities that ignite passion? Will they encourage and support us in taking the actions needed to create each millimeter between current reality and the desired outcome? Will they encourage us to be disciplined, willing to embrace the structure needed to support creation? Will our habits foster joy in the journey and a healthy self-esteem? Do we have equanimity? If so, we are ready to be an effective entrepreneur.

For the vast majority of entrepreneurs-in-training, their habits of thinking do not support success, happiness, and peace of mind. Most have a few unhealthy habits that are attempting to sabotage efforts. These habits will make the journey much harder than it needs to be. We also have natural strengths that are not being fully managed and maximized. When we do, these gifts make the journey easier.

Og writes, *"My actions are ruled by appetite, passion, preju-dice, greed, love, fear, environment, habit, and the worst of these tyrants is habit... My bad habits must be destroyed and new fur-rows prepared for good seed."*

The *Assessment* has measured our habits of thinking. In private pivotal moments of increased consciousness, created while climbing, we are going to have the opportunity to manage and maximize strengths and change unhealthy habits of think-ing. The path provides ample opportunities to do so. In these moments, we consciously replace old habits with new and healthier habits and each time we do, we toss out a rock and the climb becomes increasingly easier.

We have worked tirelessly to perfect the *Assessment* experi-ence, we have also invested years perfecting the curriculum—the practices and processes designed to manage and maximize strengths and facilitate desired changes. As the needs of people have deepened so has our approach.

In addition, we have trained numerous highly qualified indi-viduals to review *Assessment* results and coach the practicum. It has been an inspired journey with one objective—create real and lasting change as quickly as possible for our clients and make it affordable. We may meet two or three of these mentors along our path up the mountain.

It's time to start the worthy journey of becoming an entrepre-neur. It's time to move from the warmth and safety of our car in the parking lot to the trailhead that leads to the summit of Mt. Entrepreneur.

Let's put on our hiking gear, bring our book and the summary report from our *Habit Finder Assessment*, and begin the journey.

"It's about time!!" we shout aloud as we leap out of our car, book in hand. We pop open the trunk of our car and inspect our gear. We tuck the book in the side pouch of our backpack and put our smart phone, with our Assessment results, in a jean pocket. We take off our running shoes, balance on the back bumper, and slip on and tie the laces of our hiking boots. As we do so, we take alternating glimpses of the summit and the trailhead. We can feel every beat of our heart.

We stand up straight, put our arms through the straps of our backpack, close the trunk, look around at the cars in the parking lot still occupied by frozen souls, and take our first step in the direction of the trailhead.

— SECTION III —
The Three Mile Markers

Today I begin a new life.

Today I shed my old skin which hath, too long, suffered the bruises of failure and the wounds of mediocrity.

Today I am born anew and my birthplace is a vineyard where there is fruit for all.

Today I will pluck grapes of wisdom from the tallest and fullest vines in the vineyard, for these were planted by the wisest of my profession who have come before me, generation upon generation.

Today I will savor the taste of grapes from these vines and verily I will swallow the seed of success buried in each and new life will sprout within me.

- Og Mandino

THE FIRST MILE MARKER
Valuing People Intrinsically

AS WE APPROACH THE TRAILHEAD, a gentleman dressed head to toe in the latest hiking apparel joins us. He's holding a backpack with his right hand, the very one we wanted but it was a little too pricey.

"Welcome to the trailhead."

Nervous and a bit awkward we respond, "Thank you. Nice backpack."

"Thanks. My wife picked it out for me," he replies with a slight tone of self-deprecation.

Feeling a little more comfortable we initiate, "First time for you?"

"Oh, no. Been up this mountain a few times," he responds while taking off his hat and wiping his brow with a large red bandana.

Immediately recognizing him, we respond, "You're Tom Johnson, the keynote speaker at the event yesterday. We met out in the hall during the first break."

He turns and smiles, "Yes, I remember. Did you enjoy the rest of the day?"

"Oh, yes," touching our gut, "I can feel that flame you talked about."

"That's good," glancing up at the summit, "You're going to need it."

We arrive at the trailhead. Two five-foot high, one-foot thick, vertical log pillars serve as the gateway. The opening between the two pillars is very narrow, just wide enough for one person at a time to squeeze through. On either side we see a split rail fence that runs as far as the horizon.

Still feeling a little awkward we continue, "Really didn't expect *you* to be here. I mean, you were the presenter."

"Interesting perspective. Tell me more about that."

We hesitate to share.

Sensing our concern he encourages us, "It's okay, I'm listening."

Reluctant, but feeling more courageous, "It's just that I've been to a lot of events in my life. Looking for a magic pill, I guess. "

The comment makes us both spontaneously smile.

Increasingly confident we continue, "Somehow, yesterday was different and now you're actually here. I didn't know presenters were climbers."

Mr. Johnson puts his hand on our shoulder, looks us in the eye, calls us by name, and says, "Glad you could make it."

We can feel our anxiety begin to melt, "Thank you. Me too."

Mr. Johnson squeezes through the opening, pack in hand, as we continue, "Do you do this often?"

Pausing and then continuing, Mr. Johnson answers, "It's fun standing in front of an audience and presenting correct principles especially when the people are hungry to listen. But it's even more fulfilling when one of them is actually ready to climb this mountain."

We watch as Mr. Johnson puts on his pack and motions for us to come through the opening, "When I met you yesterday, you looked like that person. Wouldn't miss this."

While attempting to squeeze through the opening while still wearing our backpack, we ask, "Do I call you Mr. Johnson?"

Pointing at our pack, "It's easier if you take it off."

We remove the pack and pass it to his open hand, "Thank you."

He nods and continues, "No. On this mountain you call me, Tom."

Successfully through the opening we agree, "Okay, Tom, I'm your willing student."

At that very moment we hear a very impatient voice shouting from behind us, "Excuse me. Excuse me."

We turn to see a person rushing toward the opening. He is motioning for us to step aside. He speaks without even looking at us.

"You two had better stop dilly dallying and get your butts in gear if you're going to get to the summit before the storm comes in."

We glance up at the sky in search of dark clouds but are immediately distracted by the numerous gadgets dangling from the overstuffed backpack of this human bulldozer. He twists and turns and struggles to get through the narrow opening.

Trying to assist, Tom comments, "It's much easier if you…"

The man retorts, "I know, I know…"

Several items fall to the ground before he finally takes off his pack and squeezes through. He looks more like a frustrated peddler of lotions and potions than a hiker.

Finally through, he quickly picks up the lost items, abruptly throws them in an adjacent empty metal trash receptacle to the sound of clanging and banging. He tosses the still over-loaded pack on his shoulders, snaps his fingers at us as he delivers his final words, "Hurry, hurry, hurry, you guys. No time to waste."

Incredulous, we watch as he squares up, takes a deep breath, and races up the trail.

Eyes still focused on our peddler-turned-sprinter we ask Tom, "What was that all about? Do we need to climb that fast?"

Without taking his eyes off the man, Tom responds with a sad tone, "*He'll* know soon enough." Turning back to us, "Let's you and I get started."

While putting on our pack we exclaim, "I'm ready."

"You brought the book?"

"Yes," we enthusiastically respond while reaching around and touching the side pouch.

"You've taken the Assessment and have your current Habit Score?"

"Yes, have the results saved on my phone."

"Did you get a chance to review the results?"

"Only for a few moments. It sure nailed me. Still a lot I don't understand."

"I'll assist you with that," he replies with gentleness but with absolute assurance.

"Sounds like you read the first section of the book?"

"Yes, I did."

"Very good. Did you make the first three critical decisions?"

This time and with a little more caution we think before responding. "I am committed, but I sense there might be an even deeper level of commitment required."

"Very wise. Clearly you did more than just read. You're going to be just fine."

In search of a good comment worthy of the moment, we respond, "You've climbed this mountain a few times?"

He nods to the affirmative, "Every time someone is ready and willing."

"I would love to learn what you've discovered."

Pleased, Tom replies, "Then let's get started."

As we begin our climb, Tom again calls us by name, and begins to set some ground rules.

"As we walk together, know that I come without judgment—an empty vessel. Heaven knows 'I' have stepped in a few potholes and glue buckets along the way."

We instinctively smile.

Turning and looking us in the eye, "Here to serve you."

"Thank you."

"Let's start by having you share anything that might be important for me to know about you—experiences that have shaped your life. You don't have to share anything that's confidential, but should you, just know it stays right here."

Tom has an almost magical way of creating a safe place and putting a person at ease.

"How far back would you like me to go?"

"As far as you want. Anything that might have shaped your habits of thinking."

We commence our journey up the mountain. After only a short distance we come out of the trees only to face a series of steep, rocky switchbacks.

As we climb, we pause often to catch our breath, drink a little water, and snack as we share what we believe to be a thorough review of our life. Tom is an incredible good listener. We have never felt so valued or understood—and exhausted by the time we reach the last switchback. By now, the midday sun is bearing down on us.

As we turn a corner, the path levels out a little and we see the first mile marker. It seems a bit odd. There is a large letter "I" and small "I" and an arrow pointing forward and the words, "Strait Ahead."

Putting our hands on our knees and turning to Tom we comment, "Odd sign."

"Yes, and packed with deep meaning and purpose," Tom responds, still energetic and seemingly unfazed by the climb.

Pointing, Tom suggests, "Let's take a few minutes and rest under that tree over there."

Welcoming a rest, we walk over, take off our packs, and sit down on a log. Tom begins to share.

"The first mile marker is a mathematical symbol. It reminds us of the single most important principle we want to learn and master while climbing this mountain."

While guzzling from our water bottle, we ask, "Is the 'I' talking about me?"

"You are a *big* part of it. The letter 'I' represents the intrinsic—things that are beyond value—basically, human beings. The small 'I' means *to the power of*—it's a multiplier. This is the mathematical symbol that represents the intrinsic value of an intrinsic concept—a human being. It reminds us to value our *Self* AND *others* intrinsically—as unique, priceless, beyond value.

"When we value our *Self* intrinsically, we are more whole and complete, more available to serve others. When we value others intrinsically, we *see* them—not just their outward appearance and performance, but their humanity—their intrinsic worth. We really *see* them. They matter. We care about them. We listen differently. We connect deeper."

Pondering, we slowly respond, "I like that."

"Sadly, the world in which we live often values more highly the *doing of things* and even higher, the *rules, regulations, policies, procedures—the structure*. Don't get me wrong, *doing* and *structure* are both critically important, just not more important than the intrinsic worth of a human being. Intrinsically and mathematically it's always people first. Always."

We nod, wanting to absorb everything.

Tom continues, "This principle is essential for anyone who wants to become a successful entrepreneur. An entrepreneur first and foremost values people. They actually care. They lift and build others. AND they consciously and intentionally practice this principle."

Tom asks us to get out our book, turn to page 83, and read. We do as requested.

> Og Mandino writes: *"For this is the greatest secret of success in all ventures. Muscle can split a shield and even destroy life but only the unseen power of love can open the hearts of men and until I master this art I will remain no more than a peddler in the market place. I will make love my greatest weapon and none on whom I call can defend against its force.*
>
> *"My reasoning they may counter; my speech they may distrust; my apparel they may disapprove; my face they may reject; and even my bargains may cause them suspicion; yet my love will melt all hearts liken to the sun whose rays soften the coldest clay. I will greet this day with love in my heart."*

For a brief moment, we reflect on our experience with the human bulldozer at the trailhead—*our* peddler in the marketplace—as Tom interjects, "Og was talking about a very special kind of love, the highest form of love—agape love. Agape is a Greek word that means *a heightened level of awareness.* When we have Agape we see people intrinsically—free from judgment, bias, or prejudice."

Still thinking about the bulldozer and starting to feel a little ashamed we confess, "I was quick to judge the guy we met at the trailhead."

"Tell me more."

"He comes charging up to the entrance. It's like, 'Step aside world, I'm here.' He doesn't seem to notice or seem to care about anyone other than himself. He acts like he knows everything. My first thought was, 'What a narcissist.'"

In response, Tom smiles and suggests, "This is the perfect moment to turn to page 84."

We do.

"Starting at the top of the page 84, paragraph two, let's read the *Parable of the Heavy Bag*."

We begin to read,

> There was a man who walked through life dragging along the ground a very large white muslin bag, draped over his right shoulder, and filled with his challenging life experiences. It weighed over 200 lbs.

Tom inserts, "Can you imagine how exhausting that must be dragging around a bag that heavy?"

"Yes," we respond and then continue reading.

> A mentor meets this man along the path of life. The mentor, noticing the man's fatigue, invites him to empty his bag. He is reluctant to do so. He knows what's in it—all of his failures, disappointments, betrayals, inadequacies, embarrassments, and hurts. There is a reason why he drags all of this behind him.
>
> The mentor finally convinces him to empty the bag. He dumps it. Before him is a large stack of silver orbs, each sphere with multiple sharp spikes representing painful moments from his life.

Looking up, we comment, "Spikey orbs."

Tom appreciates our comment and points out, "There is a very good reason why we drag our life experiences behind us—our spikey orbs. These are our experiences, but we want them as far away from our gaze—our memory—as possible. We are trying to forget them, while we drag them around."

Increasingly introspective, we continue reading.

The man was asked by the mentor to pick up the most painful experience. He hesitates but does as instructed. While holding the silver orb in his hands, spikes sticking into the palms of his hands, the mentor asks him to share the experience represented by this sphere.

The man stares at it. His bottom lip begins to quiver and a single tear begins to roll down his cheek. He struggles but shares a very sad and painful experience from his childhood. After he finishes telling the story, the mentor places his hand on the man's shoulder and gently asks, "Is anyone else suffering from a similar wound?"

A little confused at first by the question, the man looks up and answers, "I guess so," and then in attempt to rise above the emotion, he more confidently concludes, "Yes, many."

The mentor instructs the man to engrave this experience on his heart.

Tom is listening to us read, hands cupped as if holding a spikey orb and then touching it to his heart, vicariously acting out the man's experience.

Afraid at first, the man tentatively holds the sphere with the spikes to his chest and then gently pushes. To his surprise, the orb, spikes and all, slides easily and smoothly into his heart.

The man immediately feels as if a burden has been lifted. He feels more whole and complete, even joyful. The same sequence is repeated with each orb—each painful memory. "Is anyone else suffering from a similar wound?" "Yes." Orb slides in. As he does so, his heart grows larger and his burdens become lighter.

With the man's life experiences now in his heart, the mentor places both hands on his shoulders, looks in his eyes, and continues, "Your character has been forged in the furnace of adversity. You know what pain feel like. Can you take back any of these experiences?" "No, the man answers." "That is correct. However, you can choose to use these experiences as a rich empathetic resource to better understand what someone else is going through."

The mentor continues, "If you choose to do this, you will hear things no one else hears, see things no one else sees, and with courage ask questions no one else dare ask. You will connect with people at a deeper and more meaningful level."

The mentor then concludes with these words of wisdom, "If you choose to use your experiences this way—in the service of others—there will finally be purpose in your suffering, joy in your journey, and much needed healing in your soul."

From that day forward, the man discovers that everyone he meets is dragging around a bag, some much larger than others. He also seems to intuitively know what is in their bag.

We look up while reflecting on the impatient peddler, look at Tom and respond, "The man at the entrance, he was dragging around a pretty heavy bag?"

"By all indications, I would say so."

Tom gives us a moment to reflect and then shares, "Two things. The word empathy means to stand on someone's path—to see life through another person's eyes. We might not always like what we see, but we can better understand someone if we care enough to do so. Our life experiences help us better see and feel what the person might be going through."

"Agape. Hmmm...wonder what was in that guy's bag?"

"Was wondering that, too. Must be something very painful. Whenever I meet someone like that, I experience two things, one, sadness, and two, a desire to give them a big hug and tell them everything is okay."

This new perspective creates a surprising shift. It feels good.

"A dose of equanimity?" Tom asks.

We smile. Tom encourages us to continue reading.

> For some, this process of taking our experiences out of our bag and engraving them on our heart can be very difficult. These experiences, which we all have in our bag when we begin this journey, have been our trap doors, safety nets, escape routes—our excuses for our current life circumstances. They help us justify any lack of commitment, consistent action, and results.
>
> When we choose to engrave these experiences on our heart, they're no longer in our bag—there are no more excuses. We've made the decision to use our experiences to bless others instead of allowing them to burden us. We're totally accountable and fully responsible for the outcome, free from the need to use our past experiences as an excuse.

Contemplatively, Tom concludes, "For many, it's a huge decision to put these experiences in their heart and have their bag void of excuses."

Our respite coming to a close, Tom tucks his water bottle in his backpack and stands.

Just before leaving this comfortable spot under a shade tree, he concludes, "The personal decision to empty our bag is an important step in making a deeper commitment to become the boss and to be totally responsible for our actions and fully accountable for the re-sults—the outcome."

"I can see that," we reverently share while securing our water bot-tle, putting the book back in our pack, and standing.

"Ready to go a little deeper and find out what you've been dragging around in your bag?"

We nod affirmatively but ask, "Before we do that…" pointing at the mile marker, "One more thing. 'Strait ahead' (spelling it out) ver-sus 'Straight Ahead' (again spelling it out)?"

"You noticed. Straight means the shortest distance between two points. Strait means a narrow, winding, circuitous route. A strait path carefully guides us around, through, and past some very dangerous places. If we choose to stay on the path, we remain relatively safe. Should we want a shortcut and go off on our own trying to cut our own trail, wanting to skip difficult parts of the journey or make it shorter, well, let's just say, we end up paying a heavy price."

"Also sounds like we might have a few more difficult challenges ahead."

"You can say that. Entrepreneurs naturally resist structure. They want to be free."

Pointing at the sign, Tom adds, "Really hard for entrepreneurs-in-training to surrender to the strait and narrow."

We nod in agreement.

Tom continues, "Entrepreneurs discover that a strait path may be winding and narrow but it is not restrictive or confining. It instead keeps us free from unnecessary and unwanted problems. The Question will always be are we ready to follow the strait and narrow path that leads to ultimate freedom or will we choose to see it as restrictive and want the freedom to rebel, resist, and resent?"

"Sounds like my dad."

"Say more."

With a touch of sarcasm, we respond, "When I was a kid and faced the choice between taking the easy way out, quitting early, and avoiding the hard stuff, or hanging in there for the long haul, dad always said, 'Do you want the little candy bar or the big candy bar?'"

"Wise father."

In far too many ways his comment is also a new perspective on our childhood.

"Let's start this next part of the journey by exploring the experiences that are in your bag. Let's discover how you've been uniquely prepared for this moment in time."

Over the next hour the terrain again forces us to reach deep. While exploring our painful life experiences, which it turns out are many, and walking the strait and narrow path, Tom carefully guides us past a very steep drop off, through thick patches of foliage packed with poison ivy, and shows us how to balance on a single log bridge so we can cross a deep ravine with a raging stream far below.

We come to a fifty-foot-high rock face. Tom pulls a rope from his backpack, climbs first, and then guides us up while we cling to the rope for support. Though the climb is challenging, with our painful life experiences now safely in our heart the journey seems easier and our load lighter.

While putting away the rope, Tom calls us by name and ties it all together, "Thank you for sharing. Courageous. I can clearly see how you have been uniquely prepared in so many ways for this moment in time—for this journey. In the days ahead you will discover these experiences are your greatest asset. With them you will hear and see things others just don't see. You will listen, ask questions, and create connections with others that change everything. May you always keep these experiences in your heart and use them to lift and build people. Never again let them canker your soul."

Nearly speechless and with great reverence and deference to Tom, we respond, though words seem inadequate, "Thank you. That was amazing."

"Yes, *you* are," Tom deliberately states as he turns to continue our journey.

As we join Tom, we can feel our heart rejoicing partly because we feel validated, partly because our burdens seem lighter.

As we continue to climb and the terrain gets even steeper, the conversation shifts to something Tom calls "walls of resistance." He tells us that everyone has one—a wall—and it holds back on average 40% of a person's energy and productive cooperation. We agree this is a lot of wasted energy and agree it would help if we knew how to access it and release it.

We have a great laugh while talking about all the ways in which we usually try to break down walls of resistance. Tom is very animated as he guides us up a rock shelf.

The funniest moment comes when Tom pauses, stands tall on the steep rocks, and talks about throwing up on someone's wall while acting as if he is vomiting on the entire valley below—blaa, blaa,

blaa—and sharing that it splashes back and tastes awful.

It isn't so funny when he talks about how we can use metaphorical sledgehammers to break down walls or when we use strategic techniques and look for cracks in someone's wall and then pounce on them like a fox on a mouse.

Reaching the top of the rock shelf, Tom pauses, turns, and shares, "It's not hard to take down someone's wall if we see them as unique and priceless and care enough to notice what's important to them and then listen. People are always telegraphing what they're thinking about—they give us little hints."

Making a peak with his two index fingers and drawing downward to his right and left, "These hints are like the tip of a giant iceberg. We just want to care enough to listen and then discover what's under the surface. And this raises the biggest questions. Do we care enough to listen and explore? Do we care enough to be curious? Do we care enough to get out of our own head—our own agenda—and when one of these hints appears, say something like, *tell me more about that*, or, *share with me what happened*, or simply, *I'm listening*."

We smile because we have already heard Tom use those words many times today.

Tom notices, returns the smile, and continues, "If we do this, a door opens in the wall and we are ushered in—if we care enough to listen for those hints. It's just that simple. If we show up with a lot of noise in our head, an agenda, or with commission breath, it quickly becomes an uncomfortable and unproductive moment."

"Commission breath. That's funny."

We both chuckle.

"Think about this with me. We're talking to someone. The person opens the door in the wall and gives a little verbal hint—a tip of the iceberg—and says something like, *I don't feel very good today. I'm tired.* What do most of us say in return?"

"Me, too?"

"Yes, and the door slams closed. What might be different if we responded, "*Tell me more about that*, or, *I'm listening?*"

"They would welcome us in?"

"Yes, they would take us by the hand and usher us into their world. We didn't need to throw up with our excitement, use a sledgehammer, or some other clever technique. We simply cared enough to listen and hear a verbal hint—what was important to them—and we were curious enough to explore. People are giving us verbal hints all the time. Do we care enough to hear them?"

Self-reflective we ask, "Sounds good, but what if we don't have time to listen?"

"You mean, like our friend at the entrance—too busy rushing to the summit?"

We're finally getting it, "…and missing the journey."

"Yes. And would you agree, we can all tell when someone is in a hurry, or has commission breath, or is using a technique?"

"Every time."

Calling us by name, Tom concludes, "Agape love cannot be faked. Besides, we can only climb as fast as can we inspire others to climb with us. AND, as you have already learned, some parts of this mountain are very difficult to climb alone."

We nod in agreement.

Approaching a grouping of trees, Tom pauses and looks up at the sky. A few portentous clouds are on the horizon.

"Let's call it a day and set up camp for the night."

Welcoming these words, we reply, "Sounds good to me."

While setting up our tent we reflect on the Hawaiian shirt couple we almost ran over when we first arrived and wonder how they are faring. Our feet ache a little from the rocky terrain and we're wearing good hiking boots, not flimsy flip-flops.

Tent up, we climb in and get organized. We roll out our sleeping bag, pull the book out of our pack, and place it on the bag. We retrieve our journal and make a few brief notes while reflecting on the parking lot and the people stuck in their cars.

We write about the couple in Hawaiian shirts. We write about the little child who looked so sad as their family car was being repossessed. We write about the impatient gentleman at the trailhead and begin to see beyond his rude exterior. We want so badly to speak to all of them. We want them to experience what we are experiencing the way we are experiencing it.

We write down the principles Tom has taught us so far on this journey, Agape love, how to hold our past experiences in our heart so we can use them to serve others, and the importance of listening and taking down walls of resistance. We again chuckle when thinking about the words, *commission breath*, and write down and underline those two words.

By the time we finish and exit our tent, Tom is already busy starting a fire. Sun going down soon, the warmth will help quell the inevitable early evening chill.

"Bring your book," Tom instructs as he briefly glances our way and then again blows on the small flame, "and your assessment results."

We turn back and get the book and our phone.

"Before we lose sunlight, I want us to read a little more about connecting with people," Tom responds while again providing needed oxygen to the small flame.

Book in hand we sit down on a log eager to be instructed. Tom places a couple of larger branches on the flame and it starts to burn more brightly.

"There we go," Tom utters while kneeling.

"Turn to page 94."

While turning to the page we ask, "Want me to read aloud?"

Standing, walking over to a log across from us, and sitting, "Yes, please. Start with paragraph one. Remember, we are now in a person's world."

We nod and begin reading,

The greatest gift we can give a person is for them to feel understood. When was the last time someone listened to you—really listened—until you felt understood and they didn't need to fix you?

Looking up, we respond, "Today."

Tom smiles and points to the book motioning for us to continue reading.

Often we believe *the gift* we give is our advice or counsel. Truth is, most of the time people simply want to be heard and more importantly, understood. It is very rare to find someone who cares enough to actually listen until we feel understood.

Tom adds, "Let this be your guiding principle. Listen. Be one of the rare ones."

"Listen," we repeat and then continue reading.

We always want to be aware of where we are in a conversation. When we are in another person's world, we are listening. We are focused on their stories, not ours.

What happens when someone tells us a really interesting story and we want so badly to tell this person our story? Perhaps we might even think our story is more interesting or more exciting. Have we ever been tempted to interrupt and interject our story? What happens when we do this? What does it feel like?

Tom stands, "Here, may I show you?"

"Sure."

Tom starts to walk over to our log, "Someone is telling their story. We remember a similar experience. We can't help it. We want to tell them our really cool story."

Tom gently grabs us by the nape of the neck and invites us to stand. "It's like grabbing someone by the neck, dragging them into our world…"

Hand on our neck, Tom walks us over to his log and has us sit down, "…sitting them down and telling them our story, blaa, blaa, blaa."

Tom again grabs us by the neck, invites us again to stand, and starts walking toward our log, "And then grabbing them by the neck and dragging them back into their world…" Tom again invites us to sit down, "…and saying, okay, now continue with your story."

Tom walks back to his log while sharing, "We may get away with this once, but several times and connection is seriously compromised."

Tom sits as he continues sharing, "It's exhausting when we visualize a conversation this way—back and forth, back and forth—and this kind of conversation happens with frequency. Always be aware of where you are in a conversation. Leave your agenda at the door before you step into a person's world. Once we are in their world, it's all about them, not about us. Stay in their world."

Tom motions for us to continue reading.

While we listen, we discover things we did not know. We gain a clearer perspective. We begin to truly understand what the person is experiencing—and how this is impacting their view of the world or a given circumstance, idea, or decision. Always remember, we are in their world. Let us stay there. This is not the time to tell our stories, but instead a time to validate their stories.

Tom shares, "I was on a plane two weeks ago. I was sitting next to a man who looked a little sad. I commented, 'Tough day?' and he gave me a little hint—a tip of a huge iceberg. He said, 'Rough day.'

"I simply leaned in, willing to listen. Didn't need to say anything, just needed to be really present and available. He looked up and then started sharing. It started with, 'I haven't even told my wife.' I'm a perfect stranger yet he is about to tell me something he hasn't even told his wife. How is that?"

"You cared enough to notice, ask, and listen."

"Yes, I was available and I was safe. It was that simple."

Tom continues, "He tells me a tragic story about his partner—a brother-in-law—who embezzled millions from the business and how he's tried to hold it all together for months while dealing with angry creditors and now he has no other option than to file for bankruptcy and he's going to lose everything he has worked so hard to create for the past thirty-five years.

"He shared he was afraid to tell his wife because she is all about security and didn't want him to go into business with her brother in the first place and it's been a sore subject their entire marriage. He's afraid she'll leave him and he's sixty-six years old. Incredible experience."

Tom motions for us to continue reading.

> This is just the beginning. If we truly understand, we will know the empathetic questions to ask. They will rise up from our heart—our past experiences. If we do not know the question to ask, we do not yet know. Keep listening.

Tom jumps in, "Want to guess what I asked my new friend?"

"I don't know."

"There were a lot of verbal hints we could've explored—brother-in-law and why his wife didn't want him to go into business with him, explore what kind of business he was in—stuff like that, but I went right to the bottom line. I asked, do you ever think about this planet without you on it?"

Silence.

"Where do you think that question came from?" Tom queries.

Hesitatingly, "You've been in a similar circumstance?"

"Yes, several years ago, I had a business fail. Seemed like the end of the world. My situation paled in comparison, but I remember a very dark night when I considered that possibility. As I listened to this man I could feel the same suffocating feeling coming back. Wondered if he was also thinking about the same thing. That empathetic question just came to the surface. I've learned to trust when that happens."

We share a moment of reverence and then Tom again points at the book.

We continue reading,

> When we care enough to listen, we are safe. When we ask empathetic questions that demonstrate our understanding, we create a safe place.

Looking up, "You were a safe place."

Again reading,

> People have walls of resistance to protect their hearts. If we create a safe place, there is no longer a need for walls.
>
> Og writes: *"With love I will tear down the wall of suspicion and hate which they have built round their hearts and in its place will I build bridges so that my love may enter their souls."*

Tom interjects with passion, "Their souls—we build bridges to their souls."

Excitedly acknowledging, we continue reading.

And when these walls come down, a person releases a huge reserve of energy and cooperation. On average, an additional 40%.

Tom eagerly asks a question, "Can you imagine listening—being safe—and then asking empathetic questions—creating a safe place—and having people release this much energy? AND we are the beneficiaries—when we care enough to listen."

Tom's excitement is contagious as he continues, "Walls come down, energy pours out. It's incredible."

Tom points at the book, encouraging us to continue.

We read.

With walls down, we discover a lot about a person. Before moving forward, always ask one last empathetic question. Often we will learn more from that one question than we have so far in the conversation.

Tom ends his story by adding, "It's hard to share what my new friend told me after I asked that last question. The last is always the most important."

"Do you have any questions about how to do this?"

"Yes, please share what happened…with the man on the plane?"

A bit reluctant, Tom acquiesces, "After he told me that he couldn't stop thinking about ending his life, I asked him, 'Do you have any children?' He broke down right there on the plane and spent the rest of the flight telling me about all the fun things they had done over the years. I believe it was a turning point."

We share a moment of silence in honor of this sacred experience.

After drying his eyes with his red bandana, Tom continues,

"Sometimes people are put on our path to serve us and sometimes people are put on our path that we can serve."

We nod in agreement.

Tom motions for us to continue reading.

This brings us to a new moment of decision. We most likely have an idea or two we would like to share. Before proceeding, ask your *Self* the following three questions:

- Do I have something of value to share?
- Is this the right time to share?
- Is this person ready to listen?

If the answer is *yes* to all three questions, we can invite them into our world and share. We cared enough about this person to listen. We heard a verbal hint—a tip of the iceberg. We ask this person to *tell us more about that*. They opened the door and ushered us in. Once in this person's world, our sole agenda was to take down their wall of resistance. We have done so.

When their wall comes down, we learn a lot about this person. We may even discover we do not wish to go any further. However, until **their** wall is down, nothing else matters. Should we proceed prematurely wanting to share our ideas, we simply throw up on their wall and it splashes back.

Tom reaches out his hand as if to shake our hand, "Thank you for sharing. I wish you the very best. No bridges burned. No loss of friendship. Again, the only agenda we had to this point in the conversation was to take down this person's wall of resistance. We succeeded and we have left this person feeling understood—better than we found them—great gift!"

Tom motions for us to continue reading.

On the other hand, if we have ideas and they would be of value and it's a good time to share and this person is ready to listen, metaphorically we take them by the arm and invite them into our world. An invitation could sound much like this, *"I have a couple of ideas that might serve. May I share them with you?"*

Once outside their world, we pick up our agenda—which we left outside their door.

Tom emphasizes, "We left it outside the door. We never take our agenda into someone's world."

Nodding our head in agreement and excited to hear the rest we continue,

We then share. If we hear an objection we simply step back into their world and again listen. Objections are rarely stated as questions, so we don't need to answer them. They are usually statements that demand a question.

Pointing to our log and then back to the one he is sitting on, Tom shares, "When in this person's world we listen—we're safe. When we understand we ask empathetic questions that validate our understanding—we create a safe place. Walls come down and we discover a lot of information.

"Either we thank them and exit, or we share our ideas—our agenda—if it's of value and they are ready to listen, AND only if it serves. When we get an objection we step right back into their world. This is the art of connection. We call this Intrinsic Validation, valuing people intrinsically. These are principles and practices every entrepreneur will want to master."

"Hard to master?" we inquire.

Reaching out his hand, Tom answers, "Let's take a look at your Assessment results and see what you're up against."

We reach in our front pocket and retrieve our phone, access the results, then hand the phone to Tom.

Tom scrolls down to the area entitled: People, and shows us the screen.

"These measurements are nearly perfectly balanced—powerful habits—part of your entrepreneurial gifting."

Pointing to the first habit, Empathy, "This habit of thinking will give you very accurate levels of intuition and support your ability to experience equanimity when connecting with others."

Pointing to second habit, Observant, "This is the one that might give you a little challenge. Wants you to focus too much on outward appearances."

"Tell me more."

Tom smiles at the comment and shares, "People spend a lot of energy trying to look okay. If we have a lot of negative thoughts about our *Self* and someone *looks* really put together, we might feel a little intimidated—robs us of peace of mind."

"I feel that way sometimes."

Appreciating our honesty, Tom continues, "On the other hand, we may focus on their outward appearance and create expectations about how well this person will perform only to be sorely disappointed when they show up differently."

"Have done that, too," we share with a slight chuckle.

While scrolling back up to the area entitled: My Self, and occasionally looking up, Tom shares, "Always know, nothing is as it appears. Always step into their world, take down the walls, and create connection."

"Got it."

Continuing, "Let's see if you have any habits of thinking in the area of My Self that might get in the way."

Arriving and pointing to the most challenged habit, Unconditional,

Tom continues, "This habit wants to talk you out of your own intuition. It wants you to doubt your worth and worthiness."

Pointing to the second habit, Confident, "This one wants you to doubt your ability."

Pointing to the third and fourth, Valiant and Engaged, "And these two occasionally want you to discount your character and the value of your contribution."

Looking up, "Lots of noise."

"Yes," we say in agreement while touching our head with our index finger.

"These habits are like a big wet blanket and want to suck the oxygen out of your entrepreneurial gifts and rob you of equanimity. You don't want to wander over to that chair and listen. Should you, these habits will rob you and everyone around you of your entrepreneurial gifting."

Again calling us by name, "If you ever question whether to follow your gut about people or listen to these self-sabotaging habits that want to tear you down, trust your gut."

Tom gives us a few moments to take it all in.

Handing back our phone and standing, Tom concludes, "Great gifts. You already have high levels of empathy and intuition—a tremendous natural ability to connect with people—even if it hasn't been accessed. Your greatest barrier has more to do with shutting off self-sabotaging dialogue in this area—the dialogue you have with yourself about yourself. Your natural gifts are ready and waiting for you—the real you—to show up and claim them. Bottom line: If I said half the things to you that these habits of thinking are saying to you, could we be friends?"

"No…What can I do to shut them off?"

"Keep practicing Intrinsic Validation, trust your gut, experience the joy and peace of mind that comes only from serving another person, and in time you'll bring those other pesky habits into alignment."

"Thank you, Tom. This has been an incredible day on so many levels."

"It's been an honor."

Turning to the fire, Tom changes subjects, "Hungry?"

"Starving," we respond.

"Let's fix some dinner."

While preparing and enjoying our meal, Tom explains the math behind the Assessment. He goes even deeper into our Assessment results. He again shares that the highest level of mathematics, that which has the highest value, is when we intrinsically value our *Self* and others.

Both of us satiated on many levels, Tom concludes, "Value people intrinsically including your *Self.* People first, always first."

"Got it," we confidently respond.

"Time to hit the sack. I'll take care of the fire. Sleep well. Big day tomorrow."

"Good night," we conclude as we stand and walk toward our tent.

We brush our teeth, get ready for bed, and climb into our sleeping bag.

Curling up on our right side we privately whisper, "This has been the best day of my life."

We hear the patter of rain hitting our tent. A flash of lighting illuminates our tent. With the rhythm of the rain our eyes close easily.

Valuing Dreams Intrinsically

WE ARE AWAKENED BY MULTIPLE VOICES and the sound of people scurrying. We can hear Tom with urgency saying something about bringing them over by the fire. We quickly put on our jeans, shirt, and boots, then exit our tent. The early morning chill abruptly slaps us. We quickly reach back for a fleece pullover while looking toward the fire.

It's our friends in the Hawaiian shirts. Tom and another hiker are nursing the woman, wrapping her in a sleeping bag. Her husband is standing by the fire, hands outstretched toward the flames, and shivering uncontrollably. We rush over without putting on the fleece.

Seeing us, Tom calls out, "Grab your sleeping bag."

"Got it," we respond as we turn back to our tent and retrieve the bag.

The inside is still warm from our body heat. We hurriedly unzip it as far as possible and wrap it around the man's shoulders.

The other hiker explains, "Found them a few hundred yards up the trail huddled under a small outcropping of rocks—nearly frozen."

Tom looks up, "Cold night. Glad you came down early."

Calling us by name, Tom makes a quick introduction, "This is RaNae. She'll be your guide on the next leg of your journey."

"Good morning, RaNae."

RaNae smiles, calls us by name, and returns, "Good morning."

"Are they going to be okay?"

"Just need to get their body temperatures up a little," RaNae shares while rubbing the woman's back.

Turning to Tom, she continues, "Will you be able to get these two folks down the mountain by yourself?"

Tom responds, "Not expecting anyone new today, so we can take our time."

Turning to the man and putting our arm around his shoulder for added warmth, "What's your wife's name?"

Still shivering he shares while reaching out and half shaking ours with his quivering hand, "Trudy and I'm Bill."

"Bill, good to meet you. So glad RaNae found you. Was worried about you last night. Wasn't sure how you got up that rocky cliff and through the poison ivy without pants and hiking boots."

"It was crazy. The log over the ravine was the worst. Lost our suitcases," Bill responds while pulling the sleeping bag tighter around his body. "Fortunately, we stopped and put on long pants and tennis shoes before we climbed the first rock shelf or we would've been goners last night."

Glancing down at Bill's soaking wet socks and shoes, "I have some extra socks. I'll be right back."

We rush over to the tent and retrieve our socks and return. We get down on one knee and carefully remove his thrashed tennis shoes and wet socks one foot at time. As we do, we rub his feet in an attempt to improve circulation and then slide on a welcome dry sock.

Finishing, "There. That should help a little."

"Thank you."

Tom and RaNae are working hard to warm up Trudy. Sitting on his knees, Tom twists around and places another log on the fire as RaNae re-positions Trudy closer to the flame.

"Come on girl, you can do this," RaNae says encouragingly as she continues to rub Trudy's back. Trudy is crying.

"Would some hot chocolate help?" we ask, wanting to assist in any way possible.

"That would be great," Tom says while briefly glancing up and then over at the small aluminum teapot resting on hot coals. "Should be hot by now."

We rush back to our tent and retrieve a handful of single serve packets and our aluminum cup. We return to the fire, pour some water, add the hot chocolate, and in a hurry, stir with our finger. We hand the cup to RaNae who helps Trudy take a small sip.

We look back at Bill. His tears are starting to flow witnessing the kindness being given to his wife. We walk over and sit next to him while preparing another hot chocolate using Tom's cup.

"Bill, have a question for you."

Bill wipes his eyes with a corner of the sleeping bag and listens.

"How did you do it? I mean, what kept you going?"

"Good question. Guess we really wanted to get to the summit."

Handing Bill the cup and leaning in, "Share more."

Hearing those specific words, Tom immediately looks up. We share a brief knowing glance.

Bill takes a sip and continues, still clinging to the sleeping bag with his other hand, "They told us it would be easy and wouldn't take long—just stay on the trail."

We lean in further, welcoming him to share.

"We kept going believing we were almost there, but it kept getting steeper and harder." Glancing over at Trudy, "We can do almost anything, but this…"

"What was your why—what kept driving you to continue?

Tom straightens up and listens.

"Long story…"

Glancing over at RaNae and Tom, "We're listening…"

"Trudy and I both hate our jobs…dead ends. We wanted something that would be more fulfilling, something that would give us the time and financial freedom to do the things we wanted to do with our children. Something we never had as kids."

"How much income do you need to replace in order to pursue your dream?"

"Oh, six thousand a month."

We nod taking it all in while searching for an empathic question.

One comes and we ask, "At this moment in time, what's your greatest fear?"

Motioning to the mountain peak with his head, "Pursuing our crazy dream and having it almost cost us *everything.*"

We want to ask another empathetic question. What could one be? It's then we remember the verbal hint, the tip of the iceberg, *something we never had as kids.*

"Bill, share with us what it was like growing up—when you were a kid?"

"Hah! Horrible!" he responds in disgust.

"If you are comfortable, please share," we encouragingly respond.

Hesitant at first and then relaxing, Bill continues, "My dad left when I was four. Trudy's dad was an alcoholic. My mom worked three jobs—never saw her. Trudy's mom, along with the kids, grew up not knowing the next time her 'pops' would blow a fuse and take it out on someone. Both of us spent our childhood moving multiple times—26 for Trudy—18 for me. Seemed like we spend our entire childhood wondering where we might sleep or when we might have our next meal."

"Poorer than church mice?" we say with an empathetic smile.

"Church mice live in luxury compared to us."

The comment brings a welcomed smile to everyone, including Trudy.

"And you want your children to have a better life?"

"Yes…more than anything in the world."

"How many children?"

"Two."

"What are their names and ages?"

"Katie, eight years old, and Linden, four."

Our mind is spinning. Is this the right time? Is he ready to listen? Will it serve him? Should we just focus on getting them healthy enough to make it down the mountain? Then we remember, ask one more empathetic question. It comes.

"Bill, if you knew how to climb this mountain in relative safety, with clear direction, and mentors who would prepare you and guide you, do you think you would ever want to try it again?"

"After what we have been through?"

And then another question flows.

"Yes. Is there still a little fire burning deep down inside your gut—even after a very cold night?"

Bill ponders and then whispers, "Yes. I think so."

"Do you have the book?"

"What book?" Bill asks.

"I'll be right back."

We race to our tent to retrieve our book.

Tom knowing what we are about to do, reaches in his pack and retrieves his copy. He momentarily and lovingly looks at his torn and tattered copy with numerous plastic page markers.

Standing, Tom calls out to us, "Let's give him mine. You'll need yours for the journey."

Now standing at the entrance to our tent book in hand we nod in agreement, lean down and gently toss it back in the tent, and walk back over to the group. Tom hands us his book and we gratefully accept.

Sitting down next to Bill, "Get some rest and then read the first section. Focus on the word, 'driver.' Can you remember that?"

Bill nods affirmatively, "Driver."

"Come back to the trailhead a prepared student. Don't know exactly how it happens, but pretty sure someone will meet you at the entrance, at least that's how it happened for me."

We glance over to Tom and RaNae who nod in agreement.

"They will walk with you and assist you. The obstacles will still be here, I trust that is true, but with a good mentor who can guide you, each of these challenges will make you stronger. Each lesson taught and learned will make your load lighter and the climb easier."

Putting our hand on Bill's knee, "Will you promise to get some rest, read the first section of the book, and then come back to the mountain?"

Holding the sleeping bag with one hand, Bill extends his other hand, "Yes, I promise."

We give him the book.

Trudy, who is gaining strength, asks, "Why is everyone being so kind?"

We look to Tom and RaNae for the answer. Interestingly both defers to us. We hesitate not knowing what to say, but then the words begin to flow—each sentence spoken with more clarity and confidence.

"Trudy...Bill, the most important lesson we learn on this mountain is that everyone is unique and priceless. Everyone! This mountain needs you. Your children need to see you climb it. You are breaking a chain in your family that I sense has been there for many generations. You are setting a new course for the generations that will follow."

Even we are surprised by the inspired words that flow. Proud and a bit emotional, Tom has already reached for his bandana. RaNae is serving Trudy and smiling.

Trudy puts her hand on RaNae's shoulder.

"I'm feeling much better. Thank you."

Tom stands, "Then RaNae, you two need to get going—big day ahead of you. We'll stay by the fire for a couple more hours, get some food in our bellies, and work our way down the mountain."

"Sounds like a great plan," RaNae responds. "Bill and Trudy, you're in good hands with this man."

"I can tell," Trudy shares while giving Tom a warm smile.

Calling us by name, RaNae turns to us, "Let's get packed up and be on our way."

Bill hands us our sleeping bag while calling us by name, "You can take this. Finally warming up. Thanks for listening."

"Bill, thank you for sharing. So excited for you."

We extend our hand. Bill gives us a warm, firm handshake.

We turn, walk over and take down our tent, pack our gear and walk back over to the fire, pack in hand, and lean it against the log.

We say our goodbyes to Bill and Trudy.

Turning and giving Tom a big hug we whisper, "How can I ever repay you for all that you've given me?"

Still holding the embrace, Tom shares, "Watching you this morning was reward enough. So proud of you."

Now we both get emotional.

Patting our shoulder, Tom admonishes, "Better be on your way."

We nod and turn to RaNae, "Let's make it happen."

We swing our pack over our shoulders, wave goodbye, and off we go.

For the first few minutes no words are spoken. We privately reflect on the joy and peace of mind we are feeling.

Privately we conclude, "I'm going to make this the best day of my life."

Suddenly RaNae slows down and starts looking into the trees that line the right side of the trail.

Stopping and pointing, "There it is. Can you see it? Right up there—that little outcropping of rocks?"

We strain to see it through the trees.

"Just to the right of the tallest pine tree."

"Yes. I see it."

"That's where I found Bill and Trudy."

"How on earth did you see them?"

"Interesting question. Harold, my husband, who you'll meet later this afternoon, got up super early this morning and had a strange feeling I needed to get an early start. Handed off my student, took off, got this far down the mountain, and there they were."

"Yes, but how did you see them?"

While making hand motions and acting out the scene, RaNae shares, "I was hiking really fast and was thinking about today and how excited I was to meet *you* and share how to create worthy dreams when I got this strong impression to stop. I did because I've learned to trust those kinds of impressions. In the silence I could hear moaning. Wasn't sure if it was an animal or a person but it was coming from up there, so I took off my pack and carefully walked in the direction of the sound while shouting, 'Anyone up here?' I kept shouting until Bill responded."

"Miraculous."

"I'd say so."

"Happen often?"

"Impressions?" RaNae asks.

We nod affirmatively.

"Always find it interesting that when I'm focused on serving people and creating worthy dreams, people are put on my path that I can serve and people that can serve me."

"Like you're plugged into the planet?" we ask.

"Sure felt like it this morning."

RaNae glances at her watch, "We'd better get moving."

As we walk, RaNae asks us to share more about our experiences with Tom. We give her a minute-by-minute review of the previous day. Just as we are concluding, we again see a strange mile marker.

Pointing, "Another odd sign. 'I' to the power of 'I' makes sense to me now—valuing people intrinsically, but 'E' to the power of 'I'? Strait Ahead, again? Arrow pointing forward? What the heck?"

RaNae chuckles as she shares, "That's what I've been so excited to share with you. This mile marker stands as a reminder that identifying and creating worthy dreams is the second most important thing an entrepreneur will want to do. It has—in fact—the second highest level in the hierarchy of mathematical value."

"The SECOND highest?"

"Surpassed only by our willingness to value human beings intrinsically—our *Self* and others."

"I knew dreams were important, just didn't know how important."

"When we value human beings intrinsically—again the highest level in the hierarchy of mathematical value—we unlock the intrinsic motivation needed to step back and really see others—truly care about them. We see them as unique and priceless—beyond value—and we love, listen, and serve—like you did with Bill and Trudy this morning. In doing so we establish trust, take down walls of resistance, and create connection. People feel understood and intrinsically validated—the greatest gift we can give a person.

"It was really fun," we add.

"Yes, and as walls come down, we unleash huge reserves of energy and productive cooperation for which we—actually this morning all of us—are the beneficiary. Could you feel it?"

"Oh, yes. Incredible feeling."

"And as we connect with others and feel this flood of energy, there is finally purpose in our suffering, joy in our journey, and much needed healing in our soul—the hole in our soul begins to fill. As this happens our self-esteem is enhanced, our availability to serve others is increased. When understood and practiced, this process of valuing people intrinsically—*Intrinsic Validation*—become our primary source of equanimity—peace of mind—and we feel it in our soul. In our attempt to leave everyone better than we found them, we are left better for doing it."

We pause for a moment to reflect while getting a sip of water.

"May I ask you a question?" RaNae queries.

"Sure," we respond while putting our water bottle in the side pouch of our pack.

"This morning you asked a really powerful empathetic question that took down anything that was left of Bill's wall. Do you remember what it was?"

Contemplating, "No. Not exactly."

"Remember when you asked about his childhood?"

"Oh, yes. Was searching for an empathetic question to ask and remembered him talking about things he couldn't do as a kid."

"Could you feel the shift when you asked that question?

"Yes. It was awesome."

"Was wondering why you might've heard that particular verbal hint? Something from your life trigger that question?"

"…tip of the iceberg," we add with a smile.

"Apropos for this morning's temperature, wouldn't you say?"

We both share a warm smile.

RaNae leans in, "Tell me more about *your* childhood."

Introspectively and hesitantly we share, "Wow! So much…tough to talk about. Tom took me there yesterday. Showed me how to empty my bag."

"…and engrave those experiences on your heart?"

"Yes."

"And this morning you happened to hear that one verbal hint—somehow knew the question to ask. You asked it and opened up a very rich and rewarding conversation—made a deep and lasting connection."

Pondering, "Not sure what to say. Didn't see it in the moment, it just happened."

"When you're willing to shut off unhealthy habits of thinking, get out of your own way, focus on others, and be present, that's what happens."

While taking a long peaceful look at the summit in the distance, we attempt to answer, "This equanimity thing is..."

RaNae comes to the rescue, "Life is so much more rewarding when we stop trying to be the center of the universe and make others the focal point."

We smile and nod in agreement.

RaNae pointing at the summit, continues, "This journey brings new heights of peace into our lives. It's also rewarding to know the story with Bill and Trudy goes on. This morning's conversation and Bill's promise may truly impact generations to come."

We have a moment of reflection while looking up at the summit.

RaNae breaks the silence. Pointing at the sign, "Ready to discover more about the second highest level in the hierarchy of mathematical value—creating worthy dreams?"

"Absolutely."

Carefully at first, RaNae begins to share, "It's simply too hard to climb this mountain without having a worthy dream—something we want to create in tangible reality that is valued intrinsically. This *thing* we want to create—this worthy dream—is an extrinsic concept. The word extrinsic means tangible, measurable, comparable, contrastable."

We look a little confused.

RaNae walks over and pats a nearby pine tree, "We take the wood from a tree, not this particular tree, but a tree and make a desk that is three feet wide and five feet long and put it on display with other desks. The desk is an extrinsic concept—we can touch it, it's tangible; we can measure it, three feet by five feet; we can compare it, it's pine; the one next to it is oak; the one next to that one is steel. In contrast, our desk is warm and earthy, the steel desk is modern."

We are starting to get it.

Continuing, "It could be a business. We drive so many miles to a brick and mortar location or we have a carpet commute because it's located in our home."

We understand.

"The business has employees—our *Self* and maybe others. It offers products or services, has income and expenses, and hopefully a profit."

"Hopefully," we add with a smile.

RaNae concludes, "A business has tangible assets, measurable value, comparable size. It is an extrinsic concept. So, whether a desk or a business, or a place, the letter 'E' represents this extrinsic thing."

"Got it."

"Good. Now, the letter 'I' means we intrinsically value this extrinsic thing. Determining if we intrinsically value a *thing* can get a little tricky, but essential, if it's going to be our second mile marker we'll want to know how to determine this."

"How do we do it?"

Turning to us, "Let's start with a thing. Do you have some *thing* you want to create?"

"Yes, a log cabin big enough for our whole family and future grandkids to enjoy."

"Wonderful. When we identify that *thing*—that extrinsic thing we want to create, our first question should be, 'Do I intrinsically value it?' If so it's a worthy dream. When it is a worthy dream, we can unlock the intrinsic motivation required to do the work of physical creation. This drives our focus, discipline, effort, and action. AND with the creation of this worthy dream in the real world—not just in our head—we find equanimity."

We are trying to take this all in.

"This process of identifying our worthy dream—our 'E' to the 'I'—is critical—and again, it has the second highest mathematical value second only to intrinsically valuing people.

The loud gurgle in our stomach reminds us we have not eaten this morning.

"Whoa, I'm really hungry."

"Want to stop for a moment and eat something?"

"That would be great."

Pointing, "Let's get over that little knoll. There we'll find a great place to sit and eat and I'll share more."

"Sounds good."

We press a little to get to the top of the knoll. Cresting, we see breathtaking beauty. Below is a meadow complete with late spring flowers. Beyond the meadow is a small glacier lake framed on three sides by very steep rocky cliffs.

A short way down the path we find a large log to sit on. We take off our pack, rummage through it in search of an energy bar. Finding two, we look up and scan the scene.

Extending her hand, which is holding an open white plastic bag, RaNae asks, "Like some beef jerky? Made it myself."

"Sure," looking in the bag and taking a long piece.

Pointing at the water, "Beautiful, huh?"

"Took my breath away," we respond, still amazed by the magical setting.

"Like to call this place *The Meadow of Dreams.*"

Taking another bite of jerky, RaNae continues, "Let's get out your book."

We retrieve the book from our pack while RaNae continues to chew and share.

"As we move forward along the path and we discuss how to identify extrinsic concepts we value intrinsically—our worthy dreams—our E to the I—it's important to establish this one critical and essential principle. It's not the *topic*, *subject*, or *cost* of the *thing* we value intrinsically that matters. It's the impact for *good* it has on our life and the lives of others."

"Okay," we respond while holding the book and taking a healthy bite of our jerky.

"Open to page 118, paragraph six and read aloud."

Turning to the page we begin reading,

> Important. This is not about chasing rainbows or becoming materialistic. This principle has *nothing* to do with fantastical, unrealistic, or grandiose ideas. It has *nothing* to do with escaping from the rigors of life. It has *nothing* to do with a desire to avoid annoying people.

We smile and continue reading,

> It has *nothing* to do with assuaging an injured ego with a deep-seated need to impress others or pretend we are more. It has *nothing* to do with greed or jealousy, or something we covet. It has nothing to do with getting something believing that *this thing* can give us equanimity.
>
> It has *everything* to do with becoming the best person we can possibly be. It has *everything* to do with learning how to become an intentional creator and creating the most we can with the circumstances we have been given. It has *everything* to do with lifting and building and blessing other people, creating

value, and contributing to the world. Second only to valuing people intrinsically, creating worthy dreams is the most powerful source of equanimity—peace of mind.

Looking up, "That's what I've always wanted—peace of mind."

RaNae adds as she finishes chewing, "The greatest risk in sharing these principles is inadvertently pushing materialistic buttons. However, identifying and creating an extrinsic concept we value intrinsically—our 'E' to the 'I'—has a very different and much deeper purpose—when we fully understand and apply this great principle, equanimity is the result."

RaNae takes another bite and points to the book.

While taking another bite we respond, "Big thumbs up on your jerky."

"Thanks. Want to introduce you to a word."

"What is it?"

"The word is Selah."

"Selah?"

"Yes, Selah. This word is found seventy-four times in the Hebrew Bible and seventy-one times in Psalms alone.

"What does it mean?"

"It's a Hebrew word that means to stop, pause, listen, and consider. After you read the next few paragraphs, I want you to practice Selah. Stop, pause, listen—which means—really hear what's being said—and carefully consider the implications in your life. Will you do that?"

"Yes. Sure."

"Okay, start with the next paragraph."

With great anticipation, we continue reading,

The process of identifying a worthy dream can become a slippery slope. Far too many have been using their gift of visualization to engage in fantasy, wanting to escape and avoid the rigors of life and the growth required to effectively do the work of creation. Others use it to engage in catastrophe, obsessively worrying, playing out an endless array of worse case scenarios about everything from fears about connecting with people, concerns about how others perceive them, the condition of the economy, past failures, and failures yet unrealized but sure to come.

The creation of our dreams in tangible reality—our "E" to the "I"—is not about wanting something, believing that if we had that *thing*, life would be easier and less stressful. It does not invite fantasy.

We momentarily look up. RaNae's eyes are closed. We continue reading,

The process of creating a worthy dream does not involve catastrophizing. Creation and fear are not compatible partners. Creation is not about ease, materialism, ego gratification, or fear reduction. Creation is all about stretching and growing and becoming and bringing a vision—our worthy dream of a possibility—into tangible reality. Let us become more aware of private and often very personal habits of thinking that can frustrate or even sabotage our journey.

In the pursuit of equanimity—peace of mind—and fearful of becoming materialistic or wanting to minimize stress, we may divest ourselves of worldly possessions—*things*. We may focus more on eliminating stress than creating peace of mind. However, in an attempt to shrink to a grain of sand, our entrepreneurial gifts will constantly irritate our soul wanting us to become better. It takes a great deal of energy to bury these gifts. Let us never confuse the absence of *things* in the pursuit of less stress with equanimity.

On the other end of the spectrum, others may want to be rich and famous believing this will produce equanimity. They may be tempted to focus tremendous amounts of energy on the accumulation of *things* believing that somehow these *things* are the secret to unlocking this elusive door to peace. Sadly, should we choose this road, pride often blinds our minds to the needs of others. Sitting in palaces of prosperity, void of real meaning and purpose, equanimity evades us and our heart is left empty still.

Some may love the *idea* of serving others but feel guilty about earning money doing so. On one hand they have high levels of empathy. On the other hand they secretly and privately want life to be easier and a little less stressful. We prove our empathy by the diligent action we take in the service of others.

With empathy we can value people intrinsically, but the desire for ease eliminates the intrinsic motivation for doing so. Should we attempt to serve others shrouded with a secret desire for ease, we will feel terribly uncomfortable and even disingenuous. This dis-ease is the antithesis of equanimity.

Looking up momentarily, we respond, "That explains a lot."

RaNae smiles without opening her eyes while motioning to continue.

As entrepreneurs, we are built to create. We have a mind capable of envisioning possibilities. When our secret desires and real intentions are in alignment with the principles of creation, we want to engage in life, embrace obstacles, connect and serve others, create value everywhere we go and with everyone we meet, and contribute to the world. As a result, inspired ideas, intuitive impressions, and creative solutions are manifest.

This process of manifesting ideas, impressions, and solutions lights up a part of our brain normally dormant in human beings. This ignites our passion and passion drives action. As mentioned earlier in this book, passion is the gift we are given to sustain the work of creation.

Passion is critical to the creation of our dreams and critical to the realization of equanimity. When we are passion-driven, we work without counting the cost or tracking the time. We are good stewards of our gifts and talents. We create the most we can with what we have been given.

As we stretch and grow and become, we have increased capacity. We can handle greater levels of responsibility with greater levels of ease. No question, this process can be challenging requiring us to stretch and grow and become, but that is the point. Equanimity is not about hiding, playing small, or ego gratification. A worthy dream gives meaning and purpose to the effort required to grow. Equanimity is the byproduct of growing and becoming.

For a moment we pause to take this all in. RaNae's eyes are still closed.

We continue...

Entrepreneurs choose to take on fears and overcome doubts—they choose to grow. They are taking the gifts that have been given and maximizing them. They are exchanging unhealthy habits of thinking for good habits. They are becoming all they were meant to become. The very process of creating worthy dreams awakens their soul, creates joy, and produces equanimity—peace of mind—the very thing we all want the most.

We stop, pause, listen, and carefully consider these words. Questions begin to flow through our mind. Have we ever tried to play small? Have we ever been critical of someone who has a big dream? Have we ever believed having some *thing* would bring us peace of mind only to find out otherwise? Have our secret desires and real intentions of wanting ease ever been in conflict with our gift to value others? Have we ever engaged in fantasy?"

Finally, we look up, turn to RaNae, and whisper aloud, "Selah."

RaNae opens her eyes, smiles, touches our shoulder, and concludes, "Equanimity cannot be purchased. We cannot play small enough to find it. It is found when we take our current gifts and circumstances, value others intrinsically and intentionally create worthy dreams."

Thoughtfully but with our head swimming in questions, we ask, "How do we know if our dream is a worthy dream? How do we know if we intrinsically value it—how do we find our 'E' to the 'I'?"

"Great questions. To qualify mathematically as an extrinsic concept that is intrinsically valued, to be our 'E' to the 'I', our worthy dream, there are three tests and one natural outcome. If our dream meets all three tests and it drives the natural outcome, we can engage with confidence and self-determination that it is a worthy dream no matter what it is."

"No matter what it is?"

"Your dream will be different than mine. Mine will be different than the next person. It doesn't make any of our worthy dreams better or worse, right or wrong. What matters is this: does the dream impact our life, and the lives of others, for good?

"How about a Ferrari?" we revealingly respond.

"Depends on why someone wants it and how they'll use it. Again. It's not the subject, topic, or cost—it's the impact for good it has in our life and the lives of others. By the way, had one."

"Ferrari?"

"Yes. Back when I was trying to buy equanimity. Was red with a tan interior. Was fast, but was also in the repair shop ten out of the first twelve days I owned it. Needed a car that was a daily driver—you know, push the button and it would start and run smoothly. Couldn't afford both the car and a full-time mechanic."

While chuckling we respond, "You'll have to tell me more about that."

"Can sum it up in two words, ego gratification. Also want to tell you the story about a dear friend who had a worthy dream that in-volved a Ferrari, but before I do, let's read about the three tests."

"All ears."

"Want some more jerky?"

"Sure," we respond while again reaching into the bag.

RaNae continues, "These three tests assist us in determining if our dream is a worthy dream. As we more fully understand these three tests we begin to understand why the creation of worthy dreams is so mathematically significant."

Pointing to the book, "Bottom of the page."

We read,

The three tests determine if the *thing* we want is truly val-ued intrinsically—and therefore worthy of our time, attention, energy, and resources. First, the dream inspires us—it breathes life into us—it awakens our creativity. We find our *Self* effortlessly using our gift of visualization to think about it, and most importantly, how we are going to create it.

With our secret desires and real intentions in alignment with the principles of creation—engage, embrace, connect and serve, create value, and contribute—we manifest inspired ideas, intuitive impressions, and creative solutions about how to create it. This ignites our passion AND we act on these inspirations passion-driven. We treat each inspiration as if it were an urgent assignment.

For example: We may awaken in the middle of the night and start pondering our dream, or in the early hours of morning, mid-day, or in the evening—any time. We focus on what it will take to create the next millimeter between our current reality and the creation of the dream. Inspired ideas come. We act on these inspirations.

We waste not a moment in fantasy playing out endless scenarios about what it will be like *after* our dream is created. And certainly, we don't talk our *Self* out of the inspiration. Each time inspiration comes we act, investing our time in creation—taking the passion-driven actions needed to actually create the next millimeter—the next little step in the right direction—and then the next. Not a moment questioning. No fantasizing.

In short, we experience:

- Inspired creativity
- Passion-driven action
- Creation of the next millimeter
- More inspired creativity

- Sustained passion-driven action
- Creation of the next millimeter and then the next

This sequence continues until our dream is created in tangible reality. As we create each millimeter we find ever-increasing levels of joy in the journey and ever-increasing levels of equanimity.

Looking up, "Give me a second to underline those."

We reach into our pack for a pen.

Underlining each and then the last one, we say it aloud, "Creation of the next millimeter and then the next." Adding, "Ever-increasing levels of joy and equanimity."

Looking up, "Thank you."

"You're welcome. Let's read Og's quote."

We read...

Og writes, "*Henceforth, I will consider each day's effort as but one blow of my blade against a mighty oak. The first blow may cause not a tremor in the wood, nor the second, nor the third. Each blow, of itself, may be trifling, and seem of no consequence. Yet from childish swipes the oak will eventually tumble. So it will be with my efforts of today.*

"*I will be liken to the raindrop which washes away the mountain; the ant who devours a tiger; the star which brightens the earth; the slave who builds a pyramid. I will build my castle one brick at a time for I know that small attempts, repeated, will complete any undertaking. I will persist until I succeed.*"

RaNae stands for a moment while sharing, "It's so important to emphasize, we don't magically manifest tangible reality with vivid visualization. That's a 'lie' sold to and bought by the naïve and gullible—the seeker of ease. We instead use this gift to manifest inspired ideas, intuitive impressions, and creative solutions that ignite passion. Passion then drives the action required to create the next millimeter of our dream in tangible reality. Creation occurs one millimeter at a time—one brick at a time."

We add, "One log at a time."

"Yes, now read the next quote from Og."

We read,

"*I will never consider defeat and I will remove from my vocabulary such words and phrases as quit, cannot, unable, impossible, out of the question, improbable, failure, unworkable, hopeless, and retreat; for they are the words of fools. I will avoid despair but if this disease of the mind should infect me then I will work on in despair. I will toil and I will endure. I will ignore the obstacles at my feet and keep mine eyes on the goals above my head, for I know that where dry desert ends, green grass grows. I will persist until I succeed."*

We look up, "It's all starting to make sense."

"Tell me more," RaNae responds.

"This is so valuable. For years I've been trying to get tangible reality to manifest by visualizing my dreams with ever-increasing levels of intention. Nothing ever happened—other than frustration. Certainly didn't experience peace of mind. Maybe felt like giving up, but that isn't peace of mind."

"What did you do when you gave up?"

"Sold everything. Played small. Lost my enthusiasm."

Pointing to her head and tapping it with her finger, "Good news. Dreams are initially created in our mind. This is where the vision is created and if our secret desires and real intentions are in alignment with creation, we take action—passion-driven action—and create our dreams in tangible reality."

Again tapping her head, "If we want ease, here's where our dream will stay. Dreams are intentionally created in our mind and then intentionally created in the real world with passion-driven action."

For a moment we practice Selah.

Looking toward the book, RaNae asks, "So, what's the first test?"

While touching the pages of the book, we methodically respond, "A worthy dream inspires creativity that ignites passion and drives action."

While sitting back down on the log, RaNae continues, "Very good. Now the second test."

We look up eager to hear.

"The second test is this: The dream en*cou*rages us—adds to our

COUR—that's French for heart. With *cour*age we stretch and grow and overcome our fears and doubts. We have the courage to become all that we are meant to be."

"Let's keep reading," RaNae concludes while pointing at the book.

> A worthy dream gives us an extrinsic or external reason for engaging in internal improvement. We are not focused on changing our circumstances. We are focused on changing our *Self* so we can gain the ability to more effectively create our worthy dream—be more intentional. We willingly and *cour*ageously...

We look up, "There's that *cour* word again." Continuing,

> We willingly and courageously take the actions needed even in the face of fear and against all odds. We courageously overcome doubt and uncertainty. We say and do as Og writes, *'I' will command and 'I' will obey my own command.* AND the actions taken turn the *lion of terror into an ant of equanimity.*

Looking up, "And there's that word again—equanimity."
RaNae smiles.

> In short, when we have a worthy dream, we have a very important reason to overcome our weaknesses—a purpose worthy of the effort. Creation requires that our gifts be present and maximized and any unhealthy habits of thinking be replaced by good habits. Our worthy dreams help provide the impetus to do so.

Looking up and turning to RaNae, "So, let me understand this. A worthy dream gives me a powerful reason or purpose to work on me—take on my weaknesses—my unhealthy habits of thinking."

"Yes, it adds to your *cour*age to do so."

"Okay, and as I become a better person, I become a better intentional creator, and I am more likely to take the actions needed to actually create my dreams. Right?"

"Yes. Now add this. As we stretch and grow as a person, we become more whole and complete, more available, more capable of handling increased levels of responsibility with greater levels of ease. We become better connectors and better servant leaders. The very journey of stretching and growing in order to have the capacity to create a worthy dream helps us become even better with the first and most important mile marker—valuing people intrinsically."

"Another source of equanimity…"

"Yes."

Getting it, we share, "So having a dream that meets the second test, actually helps me become better at valuing people intrinsically?"

While glancing at the book, "Exactly. So what is the second test?"

"Do my dreams provide sufficient en*cour*agement to stretch and grow and become a better more capable version of me—my best *Self*?"

"You've got it. Can you see why it is so important for an entrepreneur to become the boss, hire my *Self*, and improve my *Self*?"

"Yes, without making those decisions, we would never be able to create our dreams," we conclude.

"Yes. Now, one last test. Does the dream foster abundance?"

"What does that mean?"

"Let's read."

We open the book to the place marked by our right index finger.

"Start on page 131, first paragraph."

We turn to that page and continue reading.

When our dream fosters abundance, we want to share what we create to bless lives, lift burdens, and inspire others to be their very best—and share how they can do it.

Again, creation of a worthy dream is not about ego gratification, greed, or materialism. Ultimately, it's about becoming a better person and making the world a better place—for all. The desired destination isn't ease or less stress. It's living a life of significance with equanimity. So we will want to ask the question, does our dream foster abundance?

Looking up, we ask, "What would be an example of something like that?"

"Share with me more about your dream of creating a cabin."

"It's in the mountains next to a lake."

"How big is it?"

"We have three children. The oldest, Stephanie, got married last year. Moved a couple of hours away."

RaNae leans in and listens intently.

"She's already talking about having children. She wants two. If each of our children have two or three children, that would be fourteen to seventeen people including spouses."

"Quite a gathering."

"Yes, but as they get married and start their lives, most likely it will be harder and harder to do so. We have always dreamed about having a place where we could gather, a place away from the world, one where we could make lots of great memories."

"Is there anything else you would want to do with the cabin?"

"I don't know. Get away from this crazy world for a few days at a time—some alone time with my sweetheart—but that sounds more like escaping and avoiding."

"Do you believe rest is important?"

"Yes."

"Is that something you might want to take into consideration?

"Yes. I think so."

"Anything else you could do."

"As I grow my business, I could use it for retreats with business partners, team members, key employees—share it."

"May even discover a tax benefit or two, but you'd have to ask your accountant."

While wryly smiling, "Hmmmm…lots of ways to be abundant."

"Based on what you've shared, is it possible that your dream of building a cabin fosters abundance?"

Considering the conversation, we respond, "Yes."

"Does it inspire creativity—not only for where it might be or how it will look, but most importantly how you are going to create each millimeter between where you are now and the actual physical creation of your cabin? What's the plan?"

We reach for our journal and write as RaNae gets into details.

RaNae starts rattling off a litany of things to consider, "Realistically, how big will it be? How much will it cost to build and furnish? Will you be paying for it with cash or taking out a mortgage? If it has a mortgage, what percent of its value will be mortgaged, 80%, 70%, 50%? How can it become a sound investment and not a financial burden?"

Trying to write, "Slow down for a second."

"Oh, sorry."

More deliberately allowing time for each to be recorded, "How big? How much will it cost? Pay with cash or take out a mortgage? If mortgaged, what percentage of its value will you borrow, 80%, 70%, 50%? Basically, how much of a down payment will you need? What impact will a mortgage have on cash flow? How can it become an investment financially and not a drain on cash flow?"

We are feverishly writing.

"Now the nitty gritty—the truth about current reality. How much money do you and your spouse currently have in the bank in addition to a basic reserve and emergency fund?"

We grimace a little and share.

"Now even deeper. How are you going to create the rest of the money to build this worthy dream?"

"My new business," we confidently respond.

"Tell me more about your business."

We give RaNae a brief overview of the business we are building.

"I see. Once you have a clear vision of the cabin, discipline your *Self*. Do not spend time fantasizing about what it will be like *after* the cabin is built. It'll be tempting to do so. Basically, should you create a dream board, be careful to make it a target not a daily mental destination.

"Don't waste a moment fantasizing. Instead focus on building your business one millimeter at a time—one client at a time—focus first on building the business. Serve your clients. Create value in their lives."

"One client at a time. One log at a time," we respond with a smile.

"Yes, I will build my cabin one log at a time."

We both smile.

"You're taking on a really big oak tree."

We nod in agreement.

"Considering where you are at this moment in time, especially starting with building a new business. It's critical that for now you stay focused on the task at hand—building the business by creating value for your clients."

We nod in agreement.

"One more question and it may be the biggest one yet. Og even referenced it when he talked about *such words and phrases as quit, cannot, unable, impossible, out of the question, improbable, failure, unworkable, hopeless, and retreat.* Is it possible you might have one or two unhealthy habits of thinking that could get in the way of persisting until you succeed?"

"Probably more than a couple."

"Is there a chance you might have some very powerful entrepreneurial gifts that aren't being fully maximized or that need a little more *consistent* managing?"

We smile and nod in agreement.

"Let's take a look."

We pull out our phone and begin accessing our results.

As we do, RaNae prepares us by sharing, "As it relates to creating worthy dreams, there're two places we want to review. The first is the area entitled: My Joy and the second is entitled: Work. The results in these two area tell us a lot about whether or not our current habits of thinking will support dream creation—by the millimeter."

We scroll down to My Joy and hand our phone to RaNae.

Taking the phone and reviewing, RaNae shares, "These measurements tell us how our habits want us to value our current reality— how we feel about our current life."

Pointing at the screen, RaNae continues, "Looks like you have a couple of unhealthy habits of thinking that aren't very happy with the way your life is currently showing up." Looking up, "They want to yank you out of the Observer's Chair and rob you of equanimity— happiness and peace of mind."

Tapping the side of our head with our index finger, "Really noisy."

"Yes. You mentioned that before you decided to climb the mountain, you engaged in fantasy."

"Yes. A lot."

RaNae scrolls back up to the area entitled: My Dreams.

"Do you want to build your new business and create your cabin in tangible reality?"

"Yes."

"Really want to? I mean, a no excuses—no trap doors, safety nets, escape routes—a 'burn the ships' kind of commitment—a do whatever it takes kind of promise to your *Self*?"

Emphatically, we respond, "Yes!!"

Pointing to a specific habit, Intentional, RaNae continues, "Then focus here. You have a worthy dream that inspires creativity. This is a very powerful gift, but you will want to be very careful with it. If we seek ease or a less stressful life, this habit of thinking will, as a natural default, engage in fantasy. If you listen and surrender to it, you will waste productive hours fantasizing about what it will be like *after* your dream is magically manifested instead of focusing on manifesting inspired ideas that ignite passion and drive the actions needed to actually create it."

Looking up, RaNae continues, "Important our *secret desires and real intentions* stay focused on engaging, embracing, connecting and serving, and contributing, not on ease or less stress."

Pointing to her head and continuing, "Remember, right now the cabin, and for the most part, your new business, exist only up here. Now it's time to create both, one client at a time, one log at a time, here in tangible reality. Manage this entrepreneurial gift and stay in creation and this gift will serve you. Even when everything around you is in chaos, you can have equanimity—you can be peaceful, balanced, clear, and focused. But you may need to make some radical changes in the way you have been using this gift for this to be possible."

RaNae's comment brings to mind a quote we highlighted while sitting in our car reading the book. Searching, we flip back through the pages and find it.

Briefly looking up and then excitedly reading,

☆   James Allen (*As a Man Thinketh*), "*Let a man radically alter his thoughts and he will be astonished at the rapid transformation it will affect in the material conditions of his life.*"

"Marked that one."

"Good one. We can try in vain to magically manifest a life of ease, one with more time and financial freedom—even your cabin could be seen as the answer to ease if you are not careful. Stay in fantasy and remain frustrated. No business. No cabin. No equanimity."

RaNae invites us to again read.

> The three tests, ferret out our *secret desires and real intentions*.

While pointing toward the book and inviting us to read, RaNae adds, "Everything hinges on this."

> They help us determine if we are dealing with a fun idea or if we are dealing with a worthy dream. If the latter, we receive inspiration, work passion-driven, maximize our healthy habits, discover ones we did not know about, and stretch and grow by replacing unhealthy habits with healthy habits. We take passion driven action, create millimeters, one at a time, and in time, create our worthy dreams in tangible reality. On the other hand, if it's just a fun idea—a passing fancy or fantasy—we get to meet some of our unhealthy habits of thinking and get the opportunity to make better choices.

Scrolling back down to area in the assessment entitled: My Joy, and pointing to an individual habit, Joyful, RaNae comments, "Here we see the kind of results present when we engage in fantasy. We create an expectation, life doesn't show up the way we want it to, and our habits aren't very happy, and we aren't very peaceful."

We nod in agreement.

"Looks like your unhealthy habits of thinking have been holding reality hostage to unrealistic expectations and robbing you of joy and peace of mind."

We add, "And when my fantasies don't manifest, I've been beating my *Self* up. You know—what's wrong with me? Does God not love me?—kind of dialogue."

"Let's scroll down to the area entitled, My Self and take a peek.

While reviewing this area, RaNae comments, "Yep. You sure do.

Fantasy is also the number one cause of challenges in Self-Worth."

While scrolling back to My Joy, RaNae continues, "As you command and obey your own command and take action—value people intrinsically, get inspired ideas and then act on them and create the next millimeter and then the next—you will know who you really are. You will experience a peace of mind that transcends the confusion and sorrow of this planet—and these unhealthy habits will shift. Awareness is such a powerful tool. It supports your desire to change and your desire for equanimity."

"Let's dive deeper," RaNae comments as she points to specific habits. "In these habits, Joyful, Grateful, Purposeful, Persistent, and Fulfilled—again we are measuring how we value our current circumstances—our life as it is currently showing up—when life is not showing up the way we want it to, we can become disheartened, impatient, frenetic—running around like a chicken with our head cut off—busy, busy, busy. We may become disillusioned with life and feel unfulfilled."

"All of the above," we say with a poignant smile.

Looking up and attempting to lighten the mood, RaNae responds, "It's hard to find joy and peace of mind when these unhealthy habits are screaming, 'We want something different; this isn't the way it's supposed to be; this is taking too long,' and we are sitting in that chair over there, duct tape across our mouth, chains wrapped around our body, imprisoned."

"And they've been screaming," we add with a smile and a chuckle.

More serious, "You'll want to get back in the Observer's Chair. It's time to make the present—the Now—your permanent residence and then visit your mind more intentionally to manifest specific and inspired ideas that ignite passion and then come back to the Now and take action."

We nod in agreement.

Calling us by name, "We're supposed to want more—more of the clay we've been given. We'll want to make the most of our lives—take our gifts and talents and maximize them. In doing so, we shed these unhealthy habits. And when we focus on creating the most we can with what we've been given, we not only discover all the good in our clay, we're given even more clay—and you've already been given much!"

We nod with appreciation.

"Your worthy dream—building a business, building the cabin— truth is, you'll only create it if you take the clay you currently have— your current life circumstances—new business where it is today— your current bank balances as of today—and begin the journey of creating the most you can with this reality. In time, if you stay focused and passion-driven, you'll create your dream."

"Yes, I will."

Pointing at a measurement in the Assessment, "Always remember, you are the green in each measurement. This represents your true *Self.* The yellow, orange, and red are just unhealthy habits trying to pull you off center and rob your joy and destroy your peace of mind. When the measurement is totally green, you know your habits of thinking will support your efforts. Stay in creation, choose to be the green—sit in the Observer's Chair, get there sooner and stay there longer. These unhealthy habits can shift over time as we consciously make better choices and create healthier habits of thinking.

We are writing in our journal.

"Let's scroll down to the Outer World—thoughts we have with our *Self* about things outside our skin—people, work, and structure. Let's scroll down to the area entitled: Work. These are the habits that show up when we are actually doing the work.

"These habits look really balanced. You have a lot of natural entre-preneurial gifts—powerful habits—Passion: a willingness to suffer for something you love; Conscientious: the ability to know what needs to be done and how to do it; Organized: Doing things an organized way; Compliant: following the rules; Proactive: taking on challenges as they occur; and Guardian: the ability to protect what you build—lots of gifts. You'll want to access these entrepreneurial gifts and maximize them."

Looking up, "No more procrastination! No more delay, delay, delay, jump in, surprise."

We nod while writing.

"Only one of these habits of thinking has a little challenge, Conscientious." Looking up again, "It's a little impatient."

RaNae continues with histrionics, "This habit can sound something like this, 'Do I have to do everything myself to get things done right?' or 'Can you imagine what I could do if I didn't have to involve these people?'"

We both laugh.

RaNae continues without missing a beat, "Looking at the habits that drive Work and the habits that create Joy, I have one question. Does it ever feel like linear time—tick, tick, tick—just goes by too slowly?"

We again laugh.

"Where do we do the work of physical creation?

"In tangible reality," we say while still laughing.

"Bummer, right?"

"Sometimes."

Again tapping her head with her index finger, RaNae continues, "You may have been spending so much time in your head that this has been your primary residence. Here in our minds we can create a Lear Jet in a nanosecond, fly to an exotic island, scuba dive in the crystal clear water, live *The Life of Riley*, and do so in the fifteen minutes it takes to shower in the morning. In reality it takes months to create the jet alone, and only if we have the fifteen or twenty million needed to place the order."

We share a fun but slightly painful laugh as we come face to face with our greatest challenge to creation and our greatest robber of equanimity—fantasy.

"Don't let frustration and discouragement rob you of these entrepreneurial gifts."

"Got it."

"Every entrepreneurial soul struggles with the temptation to fantasize. It's the bane of everyone with entrepreneurial gifting. Now you know you can manage your gift of visualization by keeping your secret desires and real intentions focused on engaging, embracing, connecting and serving, and contributing."

Looking and pointing to a skinny trail that winds up the face of the cliff, RaNae continues, "See that trail?"

Squinting and seeing, "Looks steep."

"It'll take us the rest of the day to climb. Are you rested and ready?"

Looking up at the trail, "Hope so."

"I'll share the story about my friend who dreamed of having a Ferrari while we climb. I think you'll like it."

Putting things away in our pack, we pause, "You said something about three tests AND a natural outcome."

"Yes, I did. You'll discover the natural outcome after you and I get to the top of that cliff."

We smile, finish packing, and begin the journey. As we walk around the small lake and begin our ascent, RaNae begins to tell us about her friend who wanted a Ferrari. The story has a familiar beginning,

RaNae shares, "At first it was nothing more than a fantasy. He would spend hours working on his dream board—pictures of his Ferrari taken from every angle possible. He wrote flowery affirmations about what it would be like to drive along the coast highway and in winding mountain passes with the wind blowing through his hair. He would spend endless hours fantasizing what it would be like to own the car. He even started visiting dealerships that sold exotic cars. Once he even pretended to be wealthy and started negotiating for one. At the time he had $2,000 in his bank account. His visualizations were not only out of control, he was doing nothing to improve his bank balance. He wanted it to magically manifest."

She continues to share the story as we begin the most rigorous part of the climb. Clouds are gathering and we can see lightning and hear thunder echoing off the steep cliff.

As the terrain gets more dangerous and the weather more severe, RaNae pauses and instructs us to get out a poncho. Secured, she instructs us to tighten the straps on our backpack.

Ignoring the rain that starts to fall, she shares that her friend had a major shift when he decided to climb the mountain.

Pointing down at the log where we were once sitting, now far below and drenched in rain, RaNae shares, "Right there on that same log. It was like a light came on. Major realization."

We immediately see a flash of lighting and almost immediate thunder.

"That was close," we comment.

"Keep your hands on the rocks," she advises and then continues the story as we inch our way up the steep trail. "First, he discovered that his fantasy Ferrari was all about ego gratification. He wanted to feel better about himself."

"What happened? What was his breakthrough?" we ask just as a loose rock slips from under our left foot and RaNae reaches back to calm our nerves.

We listen as the rock crashes against the cliff face several times while dropping hundreds of feet. RaNae continues without missing a beat, "We put his dream through the three tests. It was the discussion around abundance that finally brought it all together."

"How did that help?" we ask still clinging to the wet rock face while continuing to inch our way up the narrow trail.

"He discovered how to make his fantasy Ferrari part of a worthy dream."

We look down.

RaNae attempts to distract us from the danger, "Keep looking up at the trail."

"Happily," we respond and then continue.

"Turns out he had a little brother with a serious disability who was confined to a wheelchair. His family didn't have the means to create very many opportunities, so his little brother stayed in his room most of the time. My friend discovered he wanted to give little children with similar challenges an opportunity to ride in an exotic sports car around a real racetrack. "

As we continue to climb, often hanging on to chains secured to the cliff wall or natural outcroppings in the rocks, RaNae is unfazed. She continues to share, "He went home, got a group of friends involved who in turn attracted a group of wildly successful entrepreneurs."

RaNae pauses to give us direction about where to place our feet in a particularly difficult spot and then continues, "They created a local car club dedicated to giving children rides in exotic cars. Even though he didn't have a Ferrari, he was elected the president of the club. Several of the successful entrepreneurs had Ferraris and other really cool exotics so he got to drive them all…and bless little children."

Nervous—actually scared to death—and with a touch sarcasm, we respond, "And everyone lived happily ever after."

The remark brings a laugh from RaNae as she continues sharing, "Over the years, the concept grew. Corporations started getting involved. Executives started wanting to send their teams to the track to create bonding experiences. Soon he was asked to give a keynote address about his experiences at a sales meeting and then at a convention.

Over time and with lots and lots of speeches, he became a brilliant speaker and trainer."

Rain finally slowing down and while surveying the sky, we ask, "What happened to the children's project?"

RaNae shares, "The children became the focus of a new foundation. Corporations contributed millions, more exotic cars were purchased, and more kids got to have the experience of a lifetime."

Pausing on a particularly steep spot, "So he got his Ferrari?"

"Not the way he originally fantasized," she says while pointing and again providing guidance for our footing. "With the revenue from speaking he bought a new Corvette with 650 horses. He, too, wanted a daily driver. Now he's the president of the local Corvette Club."

As we finally crest the top of the cliff, the rain stops.

RaNae summarizes, "Our dreams can morph and change over time, but the real drivers—inspired creativity, a willingness to stretch and grow and become, and a desire to foster abundance—never change. Put every dream through these three tests and you will know if you really want to create it or if it's just a good idea we want to fantasize about. AND, if it's a worthy dream, we unlock the intrinsic motivation to create it."

As we summit the cliff, exhausted and yet exhilarated, we drop our pack, take off our poncho, and look up at the now revealed majestic peak in the near distance, which is now looming over us. We can see another hiker running toward us.

"Hello, you two! Happy to see you made it okay!"

Calling us by name, RaNae turns toward the hiker, "Meet my husband, Harold."

Harold arrives. RaNae gives him a big hug and a kiss, then turns and introduces us. "Sweetheart, this is my new friend," and calls us by name.

Reaching us, Harold shakes our hand, "Pleasure to meet you."

Harold takes off a small daypack and reaching in, pulls out a welcome sandwich for each of us, "Thought you two might need a little nourishment."

Acknowledging the gift, "Thanks."

Turning to RaNae, Harold excitedly exclaims, "Did you see that rain? Lightning was really close!"

Taking a big bite and then putting our hands on our knees still trying to catch our breath, we mumble, mouth full, "Nearly hit us, but RaNae kept me distracted with stories about Ferraris."

RaNae and Harold share a knowing smile.

RaNae puts a hand on our shoulder and points to the base of the summit, "We'd better get going, sun will be going down soon and we still have about a half-mile to camp."

We reach for our pack and throw it on our shoulders. As Harold turns to walk, we first notice a string of carabineers attached to his belt. As he takes RaNae's hand and gives it a gentle squeeze, we also notice the huge patch on the back of his daypack that reads, "Corvette Club."

In the golden sun of early evening, the whole scene—RaNae, Harold, and the majestic summit above us, our experience—is coming into focus.

Valuing Structure Intrinsically

MIDNIGHT. WE STILL CAN'T SLEEP. Wrapped in our mummy bag and nestled in our tent we reflect on the wonderful evening with new friends—sitting around a warm fire, eating good food—Harold is a really good cook—sharing our unique journeys from our previous lives to the parking lot of Mt. Entrepreneur, sitting in our cars to getting on the trail, the Toms, Bills, and Trudys of our lives, the meadow of dreams, and having the begeebers scared out of us on the cliffs of life that prepared us to tackle the most technical part of the journey—the summit.

Our thoughts turn to tomorrow.

Harold's closing words from the evening echo in our mind, "If your dream is a worthy dream, the natural outcome will present itself tomorrow morning. It will be a moment of decision. It will be certain. You'll decide to embrace the mountain and summit, or not."

Our mind finally quiets and with it our warm body rests. We close our eyes and fall asleep.

We are awakened to Harold clanging on pans and calling us by name, "Up and at 'em. Big day before us."

We shout back in return, "Coming. I'm coming."

In the mind fog of pre-dawn, it isn't until we exit the tent we realize the sun isn't even up. We stop for a moment to see the silhouetted summit backlit by the sun still hiding over the horizon. At this moment in time maintaining body heat is the priority. Wrapped in a fleece pullover we rush to the roaring fire.

Harold is methodically laying bacon in a frying pan, one strip at a time.

Looking up, "Sleep well?"

Hands now outstretched toward the flames and looking for RaNae, "I think so. RaNae still sleeping?"

'Oh, no, she left really early. Speaking at a meeting tonight," he responds while stirring some raw, freshly cracked eggs with a fork.

Becoming more conscious, we respond, "Smells good."

"It'll taste even better."

"How does she get down that hairy cliff in the dark?"

While pouring the eggs into a second pan and then looking up, Harold answers, "When you've helped as many people as she has to climb this mountain, it's second nature. Hungry?"

"Starving."

"Nothing like fresh eggs and turkey bacon!" Harold shares while flipping over the bacon and then using a spatula to attend to the eggs, "Grab your plate. It's almost ready."

We turn to our tent to retrieve our aluminum dish, cup, and metal spoon. We return in time for Harold to load up our plate.

"Thanks, looks great."

"You're very welcome."

Harold glances up at the silhouetted peak and then asks, "Can I have a peek at your Assessment results?"

"Sure," we respond while resting our breakfast next to us on the log and reaching into our pocket for our phone. We turn it on and access our results.

Handing the phone to Harold and glancing up at the peak, "Hope I have the stuff it takes."

"We'll know soon enough," Harold says with a smile while taking a healthy bite of breakfast and balancing his plate on his thighs.

Harold scrolls down to the Outer World and the area entitled: Structure, and begins the review. "Hmmm…Very interesting." Looking up, "I'd say you do."

Showing us the entire graph, "This is what an entrepreneur looks like on paper."

Harold takes another bite of his breakfast and continues, "Your habits resist structure, resist authority, and are constantly—obsessively—thinking." Looking up, "What do you do to quiet your mind?"

Chewing, "I sleep."

Harold laughs, "Most common answer."

Taking another bite so his food doesn't get cold, Harold continues, "Tremendous entrepreneurial gifts, but with HUGE shadow sides that will attempt to steal your equanimity. HUGE."

We lean forward while consuming an entire strip of bacon in one bite.

Reading and checking off each measurement as he scrolls, "Disciplined: resists structure and wants you to think outside the box, be creative. Respectful: resists authority and wants you to guard your personal power. Analytical: Obsessive thinking—like to call it Effortless—the gift to be a problem solver." Looking up, "How do you feel about rules that don't make sense?"

"That's easy…I don't like 'em."

"Good. Entrepreneurs never want to be confined by rules that don't make sense."

Pausing and then continuing, "Ever had a job?"

"Yes."

"Ever had a boss who didn't know what they're doing but always needed to be right—my way or the highway kind of approach to management?"

"Yes."

"Tell me more about your experience."

We share, "It was early in my career. My boss was all about doing things 'the way they have always been done,' you know, 'if it ain't broken, don't fix it,' kind of thinker."

"And when you had a good idea…?"

We continue, "My boss would never listen or would simply dismiss it without consideration."

"Frustrating?"

"Yeah. My boss didn't know how to manage a team out of a paper bag and seemed more interested in covering up incompetency and job protection than creating solutions and innovating."

"And if you ever did anything valuable that came to the attention of upper management, who got the credit?"

"My boss, of course."

"Did you ever say anything—ever speak your mind?"

"Once," we sheepishly admit.

"And what happened?"

"Got put in my place—shamed in front of the whole team. Embarrassing."

Calling us by name, "Your boss didn't fire you?"

"Close, but No. But I did start looking for another job."

"Find one?"

"Yes, in a week. But kept my mouth shut from then on."

"Hard to do?"

"Killing me, softly."

Sitting erect, Harold encouragingly responds, "Oh, don't die on me. Celebrate. You're a natural born entrepreneur. Welcome to the ranks of the hopelessly unemployable."

We both chuckle but it isn't really funny.

Pointing at the measurements on our phone, Harold continues, "This is what brought you here. Entrepreneurs don't like structure when it doesn't make sense. They don't value title or position—they value competency and contribution. They are effortless thinkers—constantly, obsessively thinking about new and better ways to do everything—they want to engage in life, not just go through the motions."

Standing and stirring the fire, "You'll want to do something—create something—build something where your ideas matter and you're the boss and are totally responsible and fully accountable for the results. Be the…"

Light comes on for Harold. He turns away from us and dramatically pauses to get our full attention. He holds up the palms of his hands and spins back around. Like a classically trained thespian on the stage of life he carefully, deliberately, and complete with hand motions, quotes:

Out of the night that covers me,
Black as the pit from pole to pole,
I thank whatever gods may be
For my unconquerable soul.

In the fell clutch of circumstance
I have not winced nor cried aloud.
Under the bludgeoning of chance
My head is bloody, but unbowed.

Beyond this place of wrath and tears
Looms but the Horror of the shade,
And yet the menace of the years
Finds, and shall find me, unafraid.

It matters not how strait the gate,
How charged with punishments the scroll,
I am the master of my fate:
I am the captain of my soul.

Harold stands erect and pauses for effect.

We applaud. Harold bows.

While sitting back down, "Invictus by William Ernest Henley—always wanted to do that."

"You don't do that for everyone?" we ask.

Looking us in the eye and with sobriety, "Sometimes when I'm on the platform, but never out here, no. Thanks for letting me recite it."

Feeling his sincerity, we respond, "No. Thank you. Inspiring."

We pause for a brief moment of contemplation.

While handing back our phone, Harold continues, "These thought processes—these powerful entrepreneurial gifts—have very dark shadow sides that can absolutely sabotage our efforts and steal our equanimity. These are some of the most stubborn, hard to manage, bull-headed—did I say stubborn—habits of thinking an entrepreneur will ever tackle."

Phone in hand, we glance up at the peak. Harold joins us.

"Up there we'll find out just how entrenched they are—your habits of thinking—the shadow sides of your entrepreneurial gifts." Calling us by name, "The creation or death of your dream is at stake."

Harold's words are sobering indeed, but our awareness is heightened.

As we continue to look at the peak, we reflect briefly on Og's words about *overcoming every fear we once knew at sunrise and being happier than I ever imagined possible in this world of strife and sorrow.* We hunger for *success, happiness, and peace of mind.* Harold's recitation of the

Invictus has awakened our passion—*I am the captain of my soul.* Both nervous and excited we finish the last bite of breakfast in silence but with the thought, "I will act now!"

Harold, too, finishes.

Looking around at all the supplies, we ask, "How did all this stuff get up here?"

"Easy. Every time we come up, we bring a little something extra. Eggs and bacon, compliments of Tom."

"Well, thank you, Tom," we add while standing and looking around.

Harold adds, "And, when you summit, you'll be invited to do likewise."

While surveying the camp and glancing up at the peak and re-membering a previous conversation with RaNae, we thoughtfully ask, "What happened to the student RaNae handed off to you yesterday morning?"

Harold pauses and gently shakes his head, "Sad story."

While turning back to Harold, "I'm listening."

Harold hesitates for a moment and then shares, "Insisted on doing everything his way. Didn't want to follow the strait and narrow path that leads to the summit. Thought he knew a better way. Wanted the freedom to resist and resent and rebel more than he wanted the ultimate freedom that comes from summiting. Impatient—in a big hurry."

"Ever snap his fingers at you?"

Surprised, "Yes. How did you know?"

"Stuff hanging everywhere on his pack?"

Harold nods as we continue, "Met him at the entrance day before yesterday. What happened to him?"

Very sober and deliberate, Harold responds, "Let's save that story for later today. Right now we'll want to focus on how *you* are going to climb this mountain."

Even more curious, we tentatively agree, for now.

The early morning sky is growing slightly brighter as Harold invites us to walk the fifty yards between camp and the rock face of the summit.

Harold calls back while walking, "Bring your book."

"Okay," we respond. We get our book and catch up.

"From all indications, we're going to be blessed with relatively good weather today," Harold comments while walking. "Tough enough without a freak late spring snow storm."

The comment doesn't settle our nerves as we get closer and closer to the reality of what lies ahead. As we approach the nearly one-thousand-foot-high near vertical wall, it casts a dark shadow over us.

Harold points to our right as we continue to walk, "We'll start over there."

Approaching the spot, we see another mile marker. It has the letters "S" to the power of "I" and the same words as the previous mile markers, "Strait Ahead." However this time the arrow on the right side of the sign, which points straight up, has a slightly different meaning and significance.

While we stand and examine the sign, Harold pauses by our side and comments, "The letter 'S' stands for systemic thoughts that are, in this case, valued intrinsically. Systemic thoughts are all about discipline and structure. Entrepreneurs typically resist structure that doesn't make sense to them—shadow side of that gift wants us to resist structure, period."

We nod in agreement.

Harold invites us to sit on a nearby log and open our book.

He hands us a small flashlight, "Sun will be up soon. Turn to the the last paragraph on page 152."

We open the book and read,

> Once at the rock face leading to the summit, we will find a strait and narrow way.

We look up at the sign and then continue reading,

> The way is strait in that it twists and turns taking advantage of the very best footholds and previously placed pitons—the safest way to the top. It is narrow because there is little room for error. Wander to the right or left an inch or two and risk falling. More dreams are shattered by our resistance to structure than by any other cause.
>
> The rules that support us in making wise moves up this strait path are critical to success. The system for climbing this rock face is time-tested and proven. We will want to follow the system with exactness—clipping in, moving deliberately, maintaining touch points, following the directions of your mentor.

Harold interjects, "The path to the summit is challenging enough without unnecessary resistance and rebellion. The instructions given are in no way meant to be restrictive or confining. They are in actuality freeing—an invitation to ultimate freedom."

Looking up at the one-thousand foot high, near vertical wall and then back to us, Harold asks, "Did you find your worthy dream—one worthy of this climb?"

"Yes."

"May I ask, what's your dream?"

While looking up again at the vertical wall, we sheepishly reply, "A cabin."

With a slight smile, Harold responds while glancing up at the wall and then back to us, "A cabin." Pausing, then continuing, "It had better be a really cool one."

We nervously laugh.

"Hope you are not just loving the *idea* of a cabin but really want to create it."

Confidently concluding, "Yes. I want to create a cabin. First I'm building a business."

"Okay then. We climb to build a business and create a cabin."

Pointing up, Harold continues, "This is the natural outcome."

"Natural outcome?"

"Yes. Did RaNae tell you about the natural outcome?"

"No, she said I would learn about it up here."

"I see. Your dream has passed the three tests. The last question is relatively simple. Does it drive the natural outcome—'S' to the power of 'I', our willingness to intrinsically embrace the structure needed to summit—to climb up the strait and narrow way—to follow the structure needed to create it?"

We are tracking.

Harold continues, "We want to value people intrinsically—for their uniqueness and pricelessness. Not just the idea of serving them— actually doing the work of service—overcoming our fears and doubts and creating value in their lives. If the cabin has passed the three tests, you climb to bless their lives. This burning desire to serve can give you purpose and courage to climb this face. You can experience equanimity with each progressive step upward regardless of the difficulty. You know where you are going and why you are going there."

In agreement, we respond, "Yes."

Harold points to the book encouraging us to continue reading.

The bottom line is this. Are we willing to surrender our freedom to resist, resent, and rebel, AND trade it for ultimate freedom? Are we willing to see the climb as an invitation to ultimate freedom—equanimity? Are we ready to embrace the structure needed to climb and do the work of creation? Or, is our dream just a good idea or a fantasy created only in our mind in an effort to manifest a life of ease and less stress?

In this moment we know. It is certain. If the later, we will not be able to muster the courage to climb—we will talk our *Self* out of doing the hard things—the scary things. On the other hand, should we have a worthy dream, even though scary, we will strap in and take the first step—we will climb with peace of mind. We will embrace the structure and create our worthy dream in the most effective and efficient way possible—while minimizing danger—not removing it—minimizing it—and in time, reach the summit.

We turn to Harold and then up to the summit, "I've never climbed anything this steep."

"The bigger the dream, the more challenging the climb, the greater the need for healthy and well-managed habits."

"Why in this moment don't I find that encouraging?"

Smiling, Harold shares, "You're scared now, but how will you feel about your *Self* as you climb—courageously taking each step. Imagine how you'll feel when you get to the summit and look down and realize you have taken on your doubts, conquered your fears—made a commitment to your *Self* and kept it—a sacred promise to your *Self*—you have created your worthy dream. AND knowing, if you can create this, you can create anything—you have become the captain of your soul."

All of a sudden, we are feeling inspired.

Harold continues, "Can you imagine facing this peak of systemic thought without a foundational burning desire to love and serve others?"

"No. I can't."

"Can you imagine mustering the courage to do this if your dream is just a good idea and even worse, a fantasy?"

"No. I can't"

Harold continues with even more intention, "The shadow sides of your entrepreneurial gifts would bury you in resistance and rebellion—everything but peace of mind. They would want you to close your ears and your mind to any instructions provided. They would want you to constantly and obsessively think about newer, better, and most importantly, *easier* ways to summit in order to avoid the discipline and structure required to climb—or even worse—want you to stay in the car in the parking lot where some stay for a life-time." An image of the little boy sitting in the backseat while his family's car is being towed away pricks our conscience.

Calling us by name, Harold continues, "Moment of truth. Are you willing to make a commitment—a total commitment—a 'burn the ships' kind of commitment—no trap doors, safety nets, escape routes—a promise to your *Self*—one that you will not allow your unhealthy habits of thinking to talk you out of?

"Will you commit to command and obey your own command? Will you follow my instruction to the 'T' so you can maintain strong footholds, points of contact, and stay clipped in so if you slip you do not fall too far and or get critically injured?"

The thought of slipping causes an unwelcomed surge of anxiety.

Harold continues, "How badly do you want to summit? How badly do you want to create your dream? Are you willing to embrace the structure needed to succeed?"

Harold's words continue to echo in our mind, "Are you willing to embrace the structure needed to summit? Are you willing to embrace the structure needed to summit? Are you willing to embrace the structure needed to summit?"

THE PHONE RINGS. IT IS DISRUPTIVE, CONFUSING, OUT OF PLACE.

Scrambling in the dark to locate the receiver while holding an open book to our chest, we find it and answer, "Hello."

"This is your 6:30 a.m. wake up call."

Groggy, we respond, "Thank you."

We hang up the phone and sit up in bed. In our lap is the book. Confused at first and with the image of the thousand-foot rock wall imprinted on our mind, we survey the hotel room.

We start asking our *Self* numerous questions, "Where's Harold? Did RaNae make it down the mountain? What about the impatient student? Did he die trying to climb to the summit?"

It is in this moment we remember seeing a helicopter fly overhead when RaNae was showing us the rock outcropping where Bill and Trudy were huddled.

Optimistically we conclude, "Hope he wasn't injured too badly."

Still thinking, "Did Bill and Trudy and Tom make it down okay?

We see a flash of the little boy in the backseat of his car.

"Did his parents finally read the book and make the climb?"

"It was real. It felt real. It was so clear. I was ready to embrace the structure. I was. I would have climbed—I know I would have," we cry out in our soul, still unwilling to let go of the mountain.

We set the book on the bed and reach for our computer. Our fingers fly as we record as many details as we can remember. We don't want to miss anything.

After an hour of writing, we glance at the clock and realize, we are late for *The Summit*.

"That's why I'm here in this hotel room," we conclude. "I have taken the Assessment. Did it just before I went to sleep. I have the results. We have one more day left."

Excited we leap to our feet and rush to take a shower and get dressed.

Entering the convention center, book in hand, we notice a large banner promoting the book. We remember buying it yesterday before leaving.

We lift up the lanyard to which our identification is attached and show it to the door monitor. With a smile we are ushered into the ballroom.

The meeting is already underway. A gentleman is delivering the opening keynote for the day. As we get closer to the front of the stage while searching for an open seat, we suddenly stop in the isle and watch. We quietly whisper, "Tom Johnson."

Still thinking with one foot on the mountain and the other in the convention center, our first nearly audible thought is, "He made it down the mountain."

Someone tugs on our arm. We look down. We are being invited to take the empty seat in the middle of the row.

We work our way down the row, looking around hoping to see Bill, Trudy, RaNae, the impatient hiker, and most of all, the parents of that little boy.

As we sit, the young boy to our right turns and smiles and then gives us a familiar wave followed by a warm smile. We return a single nod and a smile.

Focusing forward and listening to the speaker, Tom says, "People first—always first. The next mile marker is E to the power of I—identifying dreams we intrinsically value."

Tom pushes the clicker in his hand and we see a new PowerPoint slide: "E" to the power of "I".

Tom continues, "Next, creating worthy dreams. First, let me emphasize, you cannot play small and create big dreams."

As Tom begins to explain why dream creation has the second most significant mathematical value, we take a quick look around the room at all the people sitting in their chairs and conclude, "This is going to be the best day of my life!"

The Og Mandino Leadership Institute

THE OFFICIAL OG MANDINO COMPANY

www.ogmandino.com

OgPress

2018 is the 50th Anniversary of
The Greatest Salesman in the World

OTHER GREAT BOOKS FROM THE INSTITUTE:

Today I Begin a New Life
Intentional Creation—Og Mandino for the 21st Century

The Observer's Chair
Discovering the REAL You!